An Orthodox lay theologian, Martin Dudley is an Honorary Research Fellow at the Queen's Foundation for Ecumenical Theological Education in Birmingham, UK, and a member of the International Orthodox Theological Association.

BEING ORTHODOX

Faith and practice in Eastern Orthodoxy

Martin Dudley

First published in Great Britain in 2019

Society for Promoting Christian Knowledge
36 Causton Street
London SW1P 4ST
www.spck.org.uk

British Library Cataloguing-in-Publication Data
A catalogue record for this book is available from the British Library

ISBN 978-0-281-08229-2
eBook ISBN 978-0-281-08230-8

Typeset by Fakenham Prepress Solutions, Fakenham, NR21 8NL
First printed in Great Britain by Ashford Colour Press
Subsequently digitally reprinted in Great Britain

eBook by Fakenham Prepress Solutions, Fakenham, NR21 8NL

Produced on paper from sustainable forests

This book is dedicated to my good friends
Father Nikolai Voskoboinikov,
who received me into the Orthodox Church
at St Nicholas's Church, Helsinki,
on 24 March 2018,
and Father Alexander Dyagilev,
from whom I first received communion
on 25 March 2018

Contents

Foreword

It is very brave of Martin to publish this book. He must know there are those who will say that it should be called *Being Orthodox for Five Minutes*, though he must have been Orthodox for nearly a year by the time he delivered the manuscript to his publishers, but even the title *Being Orthodox for Nearly a Year* would not be much better. There will be others who will say (or at least think) that Martin has not only been Orthodox for a relatively short time but also, for only a little over a year before he was received into the Orthodox Church (in Helsinki on 24/25 March 2018, the Feast of the Annunciation to the Mother of God), he was a prominent Anglican priest at St Bartholomew's in the heart of the City of London. Up until that time, he was an Anglo-Catholic, but very much his own man, not in the least averse to taking a controversial stand, if he believed in it. 'He must know more about being Anglican, than being Orthodox', you might be thinking! We should, however, put away such thoughts, for Martin has seen something absolutely central to Orthodoxy: it is not a matter of adopting some beliefs or behaving in some (possibly, by Western standards, odd) sort of way; it is about being and, paradoxically, becoming. In his first chapter, he quotes from the great Orthodox theologian (and mathematician, scientist, philosopher – a veritable Orthodox Pascal or Leonardo da Vinci, take your pick!) and martyr too, Father Pavel Florensky:

> there is only one way to understand Orthodoxy: through direct Orthodox experience . . . to become Orthodox, it is necessary to immerse oneself all at once in the very element of Orthodoxy, to be living in an Orthodox way. There is no other way.

It is this that Martin has grasped straight away: he has begun to *be*

Orthodox; he has begun to swim in Orthodoxy – maybe still in a somewhat ungainly manner, but he is nevertheless swimming – and trying to tell his readers what it is like. This book is very much a record of someone experiencing something for the first time, full of wonder and amazement – and curiosity. Particularly in the early chapters, one finds oneself carried along by the freshness of Martin's impressions: faith, summed up in the Holy Trinity, experienced in worship, doctrine being a kind of distillation, helping one to keep on course. It is the Orthodox ethos that strikes him (what Father Florensky called the 'Orthodox taste', the 'Orthodox temper': 'felt . . . shown, not proved'), which Martin sums up under the headings 'Beauty', 'Boundaries', 'Asceticism', 'Biography' and 'Miracle'. This might seem a somewhat arbitrary list, but it is what has struck Martin in his, still early, experience of being Orthodox. It is very different, I think, from what Martin found was the 'Anglican ethos', but he avoids such comparison, concentrating on what he now finds as he swims in the Orthodox ocean. Beauty and asceticism might well strike someone who is not Orthodox as marks of Orthodoxy. Others might well suspect that boundaries exist but, only from within, where Martin now is, does one feel what they are about, and part of that is shaping a sense of what Orthodox identity amounts to. Martin even refers to 'boundaries created by different and competing jurisdictions', mentioning Constantinople and Moscow. Such boundaries are indeed felt (and likely to be enduring), but they are boundaries that should not exist. Regarding biography, Martin writes of the enormous importance placed on the lives of the saints, the ancient genre of hagiography, the 'Sayings of the Desert Fathers' and suchlike, as well as the lives and sayings of more recent saints, among whom Martin mentions St Porphyrios, St Paisios, Elder Joseph the Hesychast, St Silouan and Elder Sophrony. This is not something just reported by Martin but also clearly felt. The final heading, 'Miracle', concerns the conviction that God acts directly now, as ever, and such acts – miracles – enable a real change in our lives, something that is both frightening and consoling.

Martin gives a vivid sense of how new all this is to him, how he feels full of curiosity as he finds there is so much to learn that is, for him – despite his years as an Anglican priest – quite new. So much *stuff*: perhaps there is too much of this! As the book proceeds, there emerge accounts full of detail: rules of fasting, the vestments of the priest, the details of the liturgy – and the details to be found in the symbolism of actions, gestures, colour and so forth. It is all very confusing, which is hardly surprising for, in Martin's experiences among the different jurisdictions in the Orthodox 'diaspora', he has encountered very different ways of doing things and is keen not to oversimplify or get things wrong (though he does and he can't be blamed for that). I hope the readers of this book – who will certainly be many, from all sorts of different backgrounds, including, I expect, some eagle-eyed Orthodox – will not feel that they have to remember all this if they want to follow Martin into Orthodoxy. There is no examination to sit if you want to become Orthodox.

It is perhaps worth mentioning that the idea that one can only make sense of Orthodoxy by *being* Orthodox is something embedded in the catechetical practice of the early Church. Several sets of such catechetical lectures survive from the fourth century by (or attributed to) St Cyril of Jerusalem, St Ambrose, St John Chrysostom and Theodore of Mopsuestia. The catechesis before baptism was about Christian beliefs and moral values; instruction in the sacraments involved in becoming a Christian – Baptism and the Eucharist, as well as the anointings, one of which was later designated Chrismation, only took place *after* they had been experienced, the point being, evidently, that you could only understand what you have experienced. The experience of Christian initiation itself must have been bewildering, as nothing apart from the Creed had been explained beforehand. The experience itself was a mystery – the Greek word for what we nowadays call a 'sacrament', but a much richer word, meaning a mystery into which one was initiated by taking part and into which one would enter more and more deeply for the rest of one's life.

It is this that Martin has grasped – just like that! His book is the delighted exclamation of someone who has learnt – is learning – to swim in the ocean that is Orthodoxy – an ocean of experience, our own and that of all the saints: 'Come on in; it is lovely here!'

Acknowledgements

Various people have talked with me about the themes and topics covered in this book and many have helped me, often without knowing that I was writing this book. Some have read chapters in draft, for which I am most grateful, though any errors are definitely mine and not theirs.

I would like to thank: Archbishop Theophanes (Jerusalem), Archimandrite Sergei (New Valamo), Father Nikolai Voskoboinikov (Helsinki), Father Alexander Dyagilev (St Petersburg), Father Andrew Louth (Durham), Father Joseph Skinner (Sourozh Cathedral, London), Father Stephen Platt (Fellowship of St Alban and St Sergius), Father Kosmas Pavlidis (Birmingham and Thessaloniki), Father Nenad Popovič (Serbian Orthodox Church, Birmingham, UK), Dr Johan Bastubacka (Helsinki University), together with Virginia Rounding, who has supported me in every possible way, greatly improved the style of my writing and kindly transliterated the Church Slavonic texts.

I am grateful to Professor Nicola Slee and other colleagues at the Research Seminar at the Queen's Foundation for Ecumenical Theological Education, Birmingham, who made helpful comments on my paper, 'I have no wedding garment', which formed the basis of a chapter here. I would also like to acknowledge the enormous contribution of Professor Anne Birgitta Pessi (Helsinki), Professor Kati Tervo-Niemalä (UEF, Joensuu) and my fellow doctoral students, past and present, at the Church and Society Seminar at Helsinki University, who have sharpened my thinking and made me profoundly aware of the significance of lived religion.

I am also very grateful for the help received from the Librarian at the Queen's Foundation, Michael Gale, who maintains an excellent collection of patristic and Orthodox texts. My thanks also to the helpful staff of the London Library, Birmingham University Library, New Valamo Monastery Library and the music section of the Library of Birmingham.

A further debt of gratitude is due. Over breakfast at the inaugural conference of the International Orthodox Theological Association in Iasi in Romania, Father Anthony Perkins from the Ukrainian Church in the USA asked me if I had known Father Gregory Woolfenden. Our paths had crossed from time to time when Gregory, known as Graham earlier in his life and a Roman Catholic priest, was studying and writing about liturgy and later teaching at Ripon College Cuddesdon. We met providentially in Oxford one day, shortly after he was received into the Orthodox Church by Metropolitan Anthony Bloom, and I saw him again, and for the last time after he had been tonsured as a monk, when he turned up at the St Petersburg Theological Academy where I was staying. He then moved to the USA and I heard nothing of him until the announcement of his death in 2008. We were not close friends, but I appreciated his liturgical and theological insights, and I would have turned to him for guidance in my own journey to Orthodoxy. As it is, I have frequent recourse to his informative and useful *Practical Handbook for Divine Services* and often wish I could ask for his clarification on matters liturgical.

Parts of this book were written at the Kiev Pechersky and New Valamo monasteries and I have undoubtedly been aided by the prayerful support of the Saints Anthony and Theodosius, Nestor the Chronicler and Sergius and Herman.

The Holy Theophany of Our Lord and God and Saviour Jesus Christ
6/19 January 2019

Introduction

'How long have you been Orthodox?' This question from my Orthodox friends greeted my announcement that I was writing this book. 'Since March,' I replied, 'March 2018.' The usual response in this often repeated conversation was, 'So, how are you qualified to write this book?' I tried a variety of answers, explaining that my interest in Orthodoxy began with the building of the Serbian church in Birmingham in 1968, that my copy of Ware's *The Orthodox Church* carries my name and the date 7 September 1970, that I once heard Anthony Bloom speak, that I studied patristics as an undergraduate. Nothing could really disguise the fact that I barely acknowledged the existence of the Orthodox Church between my Anglican ordination as a deacon in 1979 and the London diocesan visit to St Petersburg in 2003. It would be another twelve years before I came to share the worshipping life of an Orthodox parish during my six-month sabbatical in Helsinki in 2015. I found my way to a simpler answer. This book, the fruit of my becoming Orthodox, should be treated as a travel book, a somewhat idiosyncratic guide to a country that the writer likes so much that he has chosen to move there.

The writing of this guidebook has not been undertaken lightly. There was a moment of crisis in the library at the monastery of New Valamo in Eastern Finland. I was reading an excellent book intended to be used by families with children in order to teach them about confession. The beautiful, simple pictures illustrated the experience of repentance, confession and forgiveness. Orthodox children learned this and experienced it. I had seen children going to confession in Orthodox churches. I realized I knew less than an Orthodox child. How could I possibly write this book? What presumption! How could one with so much to learn claim to teach?

Clearly, I have no right to do so unless I am willing, in real humility, to share my experience of Orthodoxy, an experience that brought me – after thirty-eight years of ministry in the Church in Wales and the Church of England – to ask the priest at St Nicholas's Church, Helsinki, one Sunday after the Liturgy, 'Father Nikolai, will you receive me into the Orthodox Church?'

To use John Tavener's words, I entered by the Russian door. This was at one of just two Russian Orthodox (Moscow Patriarchate) parishes in a predominantly Lutheran, though highly secularized, country that has its own Finnish Orthodox Church. I joined a minority within a minority – a largely Russian community, traditional in calendar, language and liturgy, with a fine musical tradition. This church was my door to Orthodoxy, to what I profess to be the one, holy, catholic and apostolic Church. It is, like C. S. Lewis's street light beside the wardrobe door into Narnia, a constant reference point for me. I am not often there, at the Saturday Vigil and Sunday Liturgy in Helsinki, but it is my parish. It has enabled me to participate in a wider pan-Orthodox world that includes, locally, the Russian, Serbian and Cypriot-Greek parishes in Birmingham, UK, and, internationally, the International Orthodox Theological Association (IOTA), which held its inaugural conference in Iasi in Romania in January 2019.

It is from this double position – as a new convert to Orthodoxy and as a theologically qualified participant in IOTA – that I presume to write this book. I did not leave the Church of England because of some profound disagreement and I did not, and was never asked to, renounce and repudiate my past ministry; rather, I willingly repented of past heresies and errors (which, fortunately, I did not have to list) and embraced Orthodox faith and practice. This book – *Being Orthodox* rather than the more tentative *Becoming Orthodox* that I had proposed at first – comes out of that experience. It is a convert's view. Cradle Orthodox may indeed see it differently and still find me presumptuous. I was principally drawn to Orthodoxy by its unequivocal profession of faith in God the Holy Trinity. Father Nikolai Voskoboinikov was kind enough to say publicly, on the last Sunday of my sabbatical, that I love God *like an*

Orthodox. I recognized that he had perceived in me something that I had not yet seen, nor did I immediately grasp the consequence – that if you love God in that way, it is best *to be Orthodox*.

Being Orthodox begins with God in Unity and Trinity rather than with the history of Orthodoxy, which is easily to be found in other introductory books. It immediately takes us into a Christian environment in which individual faith and the Church's profession of faith interact and there is no clear distinction between prayer, worship and theology. Theology is talk about God – not as an academic discipline but as a vital constituent of Orthodox faith – and it cannot be separated from living in and for God. Those who guide the talk and are spiritual exemplars, the authorities to which Orthodoxy refers, are those whose representations are to be found in the icons that are such an essential part of Orthodox life. Divine unity is to be found in the inner unity of the Church. The second chapter, 'The Orthodox ethos', is my own statement of what makes Orthodoxy different: one in which I try to escape the usual classification of Orthodox religious characteristics (Scripture, tradition, Fathers, Hesychasm, liturgy and so on) and reflect on my own experience. One of the excursions undertaken by IOTA participants in Romania was to see the painted monastery church at Voronet. Known as the 'Sistine Chapel of the East', it was begun in 1488 and completed in the mid-sixteenth century. It is painted in bright and intense colours inside and out, with hundreds of well-preserved figures. The nun who addressed the group helped us to make some sense of the vast iconographic scheme depicting the history of salvation in a way that is both local (local events and saints) and cosmic (as in the Last Judgement on the external west wall). Without such a guide, we would have struggled to make sense of it as so many aspects of the faith were depicted and related to other aspects. It is a huge visual theology and one example of how the interaction of Bible, tradition, liturgy, spirituality, history and place combine to form a complex whole. My third chapter, 'The wedding garment' (a reference to the parable of Jesus in Matthew 22) probably needs to be looked at in the same way. It is an exploration of a given theme, that of repentance, intended to demonstrate this complex interaction, bringing together aspects of faith and practice. It is, it might be said, an Orthodox version of those matters that are set out in the Exhortations in the Anglican Book of Common Prayer in which the priest urges those who would receive Holy Communion to 'come holy and clean to such a heavenly Feast, in the marriage-garment required by God in holy Scripture'.

The following three chapters ('Heaven on earth', 'The holy icons' and 'The Holy Liturgy') are all concerned with worship: the place (the church or temple), the participants (the faithful, the saints and the angels) and the liturgical structure (words and actions). Music is an essential part of Orthodox services and the relation of musicians to the Church they serve is in itself of interest, especially, for example, that of Tchaikovsky, as set out in his correspondence with Madame von Meck. In Chapter 7, 'Music and musicians', I have, therefore, stayed largely within the Russian world as it is the one that I know best and has also produced the best-known Orthodox church music. The examination of Orthodoxy and culture, largely in the Russian world, continues in Chapter 8, 'Orthodoxy and literature', for it is in novels, poetry and biography that we discover the weft of the fabric of Orthodoxy, the colour and pattern of lived religion that is tightly bound to the warp of liturgy and doctrine. Chapter 9, 'Fasting, confession and prayer', returns us to the religious life of the Orthodox Christian and three of its distinctive features, while Chapter 10, 'The resurrection life', brings us back to the principle, constantly enunciated in the Church's life, that through Christ's Incarnation and Resurrection we share in the divine life and expect the day of our own resurrection. Two appendices are intended to address the initial strangeness of Orthodoxy, the first dealing with the calendar, the date of Easter and the church year, and the second a glossary of terms, in liturgy and spirituality, many of which have no Western Christian equivalent.

A guidebook is necessarily limited in its scope. This one reflects my own journey to Orthodoxy and those features of the Orthodox Church that have become particularly significant for me. Some guidebooks claim to show you what others only tell you. It is not possible to 'show' Orthodoxy in a book, nor can it be grasped in any meaningful way in a few visits to its outposts. To understand Orthodoxy, it is necessary to think and act as the Orthodox do, suspending the Western analytical sense and allowing free rein to the synthetic tendency, to that which detects a unity and perceives, however dimly, the interaction of the parts. The Orthodox Church is indelibly marked by the One who is its origin and source. As we move constantly between Unity and Trinity in God, so we must move between the parts and the whole in the Church, the whole being infinitely more than the sum of the parts. To perceive this, to be grasped by it, to be unable to free oneself from it, this what it is to be Orthodox.

1

Blessed is our God

'I understand that you are on the way to becoming Orthodox,' the nun Mother Thekla wrote to an intended convert. She continued:

I know nothing about you, beyond the fact that you are English. Before we go any further, there is one point I should make clear. I have not been told why you are about to convert, but I assure you there is no point whatsoever if it is for negative reasons. You will find as much 'wrong' (if not more) in Orthodoxy as in the Anglican or Roman Churches. So – the first point is, are you prepared to face lies, hypocrisy, evil and all the rest, just as much in Orthodoxy as in any other religion or denomination?

Deeply aware of the many misguided reasons people have for becoming Orthodox, she continued her questioning:

Are you expecting a kind of earthly paradise with plenty of incense and the right kind of music? Do you expect to go straight to heaven if you cross yourself slowly, pompously and in the correct form from the right side? Have you a cookery book with all the authentic Russian recipes for Easter festivities? Are you an expert in kissing three times on every possible or improper occasion? Can you prostrate elegantly without dropping a variety of stationery out of your pockets?

The straight-talking Mother Thekla is best known as the spiritual mother of the composer John Tavener, who had been prepared for reception into the Orthodox Church by another significant spiritual teacher, Metropolitan Anthony Bloom, the bishop of the

Russian Diocese of Sourozh, based in London. In his conversations, Bloom tried to ensure that Tavener was not simply attracted by icons and music, and the composer recalled that he suggested the Metropolitan was inclined to be a Quaker, preferring a bare meeting room and silence. Metropolitan Anthony protested that this was, of course, not the case but, for him, God was the meaning, the centre, the ultimately attractive force in the Orthodox Church and the rest lost its meaning if the centre was displaced.

There are three main areas that are likely to bring the non-Orthodox into sympathetic contact with Orthodoxy; these are icons, music and literature. For many they can be narrowed down to Rublev (*The Trinity*), Tchaikovsky (*The Liturgy of St John Chrysostom*) or Rachmaninov (the so-called 'Vespers') and Dostoevsky (*The Brothers Karamazov*) with his fictional creation, Elder Zosima. All of these have a place in the large, rich experience of Orthodoxy, but they are not where the Orthodox faith begins. They are too narrow a base. Mother Thekla had more questions for the convert:

Are you prepared, in all humility, to understand that you will never, in this life, know beyond Faith; that Faith means accepting the Truth without proof. Faith and knowledge are the ultimate contradiction – and the ultimate absorption into each other. Living Orthodoxy is based on paradox, which is carried on into worship – private or public. We know because we believe and we believe because we know. Above all, are you prepared to accept all things as from God?

Orthodox Christians believe in one God. They do not do this in an abstract, intellectual, distracted way. They do it with conviction, with enthusiasm, with passion. With St John of Damascus, after his initial discussion, in his *Exact Exposition of the Orthodox Faith*, of how it is that we might know God and even be able to say something about Him, Orthodox Christians declare, '*therefore*, we believe in one God'. The word 'therefore' embraces what the Damascene has said about the limits of knowledge, for not all things are unknowable, nor are they all knowable, as not all things are inexpressible and not all are capable of expression. John pours out words: God is one principle, without beginning, uncreated, unbegotten, indestructible and immortal, eternal, unlimited, uncircumscribed, unbounded, infinite in power, simple, uncompounded, incorporeal, unchanging, unaffected, unchangeable, inalterate, invisible . . . He has not yet ended, but the long list concludes with a statement that moves us from philosophical theology to the believer's engagement with God: 'We believe in Father and Son and Holy Spirit *in whom we have been baptized.*' Prayer, says St Gregory of Sinai (d. 1346), is the manifestation of baptism. In baptism, the image and likeness of God is restored and true prayer, as Metropolitan Kallistos Ware teaches, signifies the rediscovery and manifestation of baptismal grace; the aim of the Christian life is the return to the perfect grace conferred by the Spirit at the beginning in the sacrament of baptism. There is no halfway house. The Russian theologian Pavel Florensky expressed it well:

The Orthodox taste, the Orthodox temper, is felt, but it is not subject to arithmetical calculation. Orthodoxy is shown, not proved. That is why there is only one way to understand Orthodoxy: through direct experience . . . To become Orthodox, it is necessary to immerse oneself all at once in the very element of Orthodoxy, to begin living in an Orthodox way. There is no other way.

The Orthodox Christian begins every day with God. Metropolitan Gregory Postnikov of St Petersburg taught in his book *A Day of Holy Life*, first published in 1854, that we should rise swiftly from bed and, without any delay, say, 'In the name of the Father, and of the Son, and of the Holy Spirit' while making the sign of the cross, followed by 'Lord Jesus Christ, Son of God, have mercy on me, a sinner.' Then we should wash immediately and dress in a way that befits a respectable person – that is to say, in a way that is appropriate to what we are going to do next, which is stand before God with our morning prayers. The opening instruction in a popular Russian prayer book makes it clear that, as we pray, we stand before

God and so we should stand reverentially. Reverence, piety and fear of God are all ways of expressing a basic attitude towards God. The morning prayer continues:

> In the Name of the Father, and of the Son,
> and of the Holy Spirit. Amen.
> O Heavenly King, Comforter, Spirit of
> Truth . . .
> Holy God, Holy Mighty, Holy Immortal,
> have mercy on us. (*Thrice*)
> Glory to the Father, and to the Son, and to
> the Holy Spirit; both now and ever,
> and unto the ages of ages. Amen.
> O Most Holy Trinity, have mercy on us.

The Orthodox Christian adopts an open and forthright attitude to God, but without any informality. God is to be worshipped and glorified, but from God we can ask, and expect to receive, mercy. It will become apparent in due course why this is necessary, but here, at the beginning, we are concerned with God, understood as both One and Three, as Unity and Trinity. We are straight into theology in the proper sense. Nearly all the texts used here are liturgical, drawn from the annual and daily cycles of services. The Orthodox liturgy (by which I mean all the church services, the daily offices and vigils, as well as the Eucharistic Liturgy) has maintained continuity through time and is the principal vehicle for the transmission of the Orthodox Christian faith. As Abbot Gregorios of a monastery on Holy Mount Athos reminded his monks, 'If you want to learn Orthodox theology, you will find it in the service books of the Church.' You will find it, but you will have to look for it, as it is contained, in the words of liturgical scholar Alexander Schmemann, in 27 hefty volumes!

The Holy Trinity

In the Anglican Book of Common Prayer, first used in 1549, there is a Confession of Christian faith, commonly but erroneously called the Creed of St Athanasius or, from its opening words in Latin, *Quicunque vult* ('Whosoever will be saved'). It was probably written in Latin sometime after 428. It is not recognized as a creed in the Orthodox Church because it was never agreed by a Council, but, with the removal of the reference to Spirit proceeding from the Father and the Son (the Filioque), it appeared in Russian service books from 1647 (having been favoured in Kiev by the Metropolitan, the Paris-educated Peter Mogila) and in the Greek office book, the *Horologion*, from the end of the eighteenth century. It declares the Catholic faith as being that:

> We worship one God in Trinity, and Trinity
>   in Unity;
> Neither confounding the Persons, nor
>   dividing the Substance.
> For there is one Person of the Father,
>   another of the Son, and another of
>   the Holy Ghost.
> But the Godhead of the Father, of the Son,
>   and of the Holy Ghost is all one, the
>   Glory equal, the Majesty co-eternal.

The nature of God is revealed to us as Unity and Trinity. The word 'revealed' is important. The Trinity is not a clever philosophical or theological solution to a problem; rather, it is the divine nature as shown to us by Jesus the Christ. As we think about the Unity of God and about God as Father, Son and Spirit, we will constantly move between the Unity and the Trinity. Before the Cappadocian Fathers of the fourth century, writers avoided technical terms such as *prosopon* (person) and *hypostasis* and preferred instead to speak of 'three' and 'one'. *Hypostasis* is a Greek word with a variety of meanings. The most basic is that of an objective reality as opposed to an illusion. In theology, it comes to mean 'being' or 'substantial reality'. It develops quite naturally to mean 'individual reality'. Each of the Holy Trinity is a hypostasis, meaning a 'Person'. Western theologians translated *hypostasis* as 'substance' and thought that Eastern theologians found three substances in God, rather than three Persons, which would lead to tritheism – belief in three gods. The Western theologians were mistaken, but translation of technical terms has nearly always given rise to misunderstandings. From the Council of Constantinople in 381, the standard doctrine of the Holy Trinity was 'Three Hypostases in one Ousia', rendered in the English version of the liturgy as 'three self-dependent Persons in one Nature'. Both terms – 'Person' and 'hypostasis' – were used without prejudice or partiality after that date, but 'Person' was generally preferred in English and the word 'substance' was generally used of the divine nature.

Some translations of liturgical texts have returned to the term 'hypostasis'. We can read in a 2014 translation of the *Pentecostarion* – the book containing texts from Easter Day to Pentecost and the Sunday of All Saints – 'O Father Almighty, the Word and the Spirit, one Nature in three Hypostases united, transcending essence and supremely Divine!' This version, from the Greek Holy Transfiguration monastery in Boston, Massachusetts, seeks rather unsuccessfully to establish the original meanings of Greek words and uses, in addition to 'hypostases', a technical vocabulary that speaks of the 'uncommingled Unity' of the Trinity, the 'Thearchy' of God and the 'consubstantial Effulgence' of Christ. It also describes the Son and Spirit as 'equipotent' with the Father, and speaks of 'the undivided Nature, which is undividely divided into three Persons'.

One of the things this certainly demonstrates is that the Trinity, being itself beyond understanding, can only be described by using a multiplicity of different terms, including the metaphorical and poetical, and such description strains the possibilities of human language. As Apollinarius wrote to Basil the Great in the second half of the fourth century, 'each is interwoven and unitary; identical with difference; different in identity. One has to strain language, which is inadequate for an explanation of the reality.' The theology that is found in the poetry of the liturgy is not a precisely formulated dogmatic theology made up of propositions. A favourite liturgical image of God, for example, is that of the sun. Using this analogy, the Trinity is described as consisting of three Suns with but one single Light, a Light that remains undivided though it shines in the three rays of the Persons. It is a threefold radiance, both Light and Lights. The *Pentecostarion* dramatically addresses the 'God of Three Suns', the 'Three-Sun Godhead', the 'Triple-Sun' and the 'Unity of three suns' and speaks of 'Trinal Radiance'. The movement between Trinity and Unity is well expressed in a text from the *Lenten Triodion*, the volume containing the offices used in Great Lent, provided for Mattins on the Saturday of the Dead:

> In my thought I distinguish three Persons within the simplicity of the divine Oneness, and at the same time I join them together; for shining forth in threefold radiance with the swiftness of lightning, the Godhead is made manifest as Unity.

St Gregory of Nazianzus, the fourth-century Cappadocian Father known as 'the Theologian', wrote:

> No sooner do I conceive of the One than I am illumined by the splendour of the Three; no sooner do I distinguish them than I am carried back to the One. When I think of any One of the Three I think of Him as the whole and my eyes are filled, and the greater part of what I am thinking escapes me. I cannot grasp the greatness of that One so as to attribute a greater greatness to the rest. When I contemplate the Three together, I see but one torch, and cannot divide or measure out the undivided Light.
> (Oration 40, On Holy Baptism, 41)

Orthodox prayer moves between the Unity and the Persons. It does not find this easy and the difficulty is openly acknowledged. On the Saturday of the Dead, a text declares, 'Strange it is that the Godhead should be One and Three, fully present in each single person without division.' This strangeness is important. One patristic scholar observed that the problem for theological language was that of giving clear expression 'to this divine paradox which was also a Christian truth'. If the Trinity ceases to be strange and paradoxical, if we think we have understood and sorted it out in our minds, we will always be wrong. The strangeness does not mean that we cannot talk about God, but our talk never exhausts and never comprehends that which we are talking about. There is always something more.

There has to be a constant movement between the Three and the One. The Unity is vital. There is one power, one will, one energy, one single Godhead. God is single in Essence and in Nature, there is one Lordship and one Kingdom (of God), one thrice-holy God, yet the one sovereign Principle is divided in three Persons. Orthodox doctrine teaches that the three have concrete, independent, objective existence, confuting those who regard them as merely different names for the same thing, as well as those, known as unitarians, who regard the second and third as abstract qualities possessed by the first, or else as impersonal influences that derive from the will of the first. The three Persons are the Father, the Son and the Holy Spirit (or Holy Ghost). The Father has no beginning and is specifically described as 'not begotten'. The Son is begotten and co-eternal, differentiated from the Spirit as 'not proceeding'. The Spirit proceeds from the Father and shines forth. As the edited Athanasian Creed expresses it:

The Father is made of none, neither created, nor begotten.
The Son is of the Father alone; not made, nor created, but begotten.
Likewise also the Holy Ghost is of the Father; neither made, nor created, nor begotten, but proceeding.

To whom, then, is Orthodox prayer addressed? Many prayers in the liturgy are addressed simply to God and have a Trinitarian conclusion of the form, 'For to you belong all glory, honour and worship, Father, Son and Holy Spirit, now and for ever, and to the ages of ages. Amen.'

Some are addressed to Christ, such as the prayer before communion beginning, 'Give heed, Lord Jesus Christ our God, from your holy dwelling-place', and some, such as the daily prayer, 'Heavenly

King, Advocate, Spirit of truth', are addressed to the Holy Spirit. We can see that some of the prayers which open with salutations such as 'Master, Lord our God' and 'Lord, our God, dwelling on high' are actually addressed to God the Father and may contain references to the sending of *Your* only-begotten Son and to divine activity taking place by the power of *Your* Holy Spirit.

The point must be re-emphasized that the consideration in prayer or theology of one of the Persons will always bring us back to the Trinity, but the Father is, we might say, the defining Person. The Son is eternally begotten of the Father. The Spirit proceeds from the Father alone.

The qualities or properties of the divine nature are indicated many times and in many ways in liturgical prayer. First, this is done in a negative or apophatic way, pointing to the limitation of all language applied to God. God is ineffable, incomprehensible, invisible and inconceivable. God's might is beyond compare, His glory beyond understanding, His mercy without measure, and His love for humankind is beyond all telling. Then we find more descriptive material. God is at rest in the holy place, hymned by the Seraphim and glorified by the Cherubim; He has set orders and armies of angels and archangels in heaven to minister to His glory. God brought the universe into being out of non-existence (the state of not-being) and created humankind according to the divine image and likeness. God dwells on high and beholds all things below. More specific divine action is presented in the celebration of the liturgical year with its fasts and feasts.

The Orthodox doctrine of God the Holy Trinity might be expressed succinctly by combining a number of texts from the *Triodion*. Together they make a sort of confession of faith that is also a prayer. The 'great thrice-holy hymn' referred to here, and the Cherubic Hymn of the Liturgy, is the one found in the prophet's vision of heaven in Isaiah, chapter 6.

> Undivided in essence,
> unconfused in Persons,
> I confess thee as God:

Triune Deity,
one in Kingship and Throne;
and to Thee I raise the great thrice-holy
        hymn
that is sung on high.

We glorify Thee, O Trinity, the one God.
Holy, holy, holy, art Thou:
Father, Son and Spirit,
simple Essence and Unity,
worshipped forever.

O simple and undivided Trinity,
O holy and consubstantial Unity.
Thou art praised as Light and Lights,
one Holy and three Holies.
Sing, O my soul,
and glorify Life and Lives, the God of all.

The Trinity is one God:
the Father is not begotten like the Son,
nor does the Son proceed like the Spirit,
but each keeps his distinctive properties;
and I glorify the Three as Light and God for
        ever.

Unity in Three Persons,
supreme in Godhead and surpassing all
        perfection,
Father unbegotten, Son only-begotten,
Spirit proceeding from the Father
and made manifest through the Son:
single in Essence and in Nature,
one Lordship and one Kingdom,
save us all.

Let us fall down and worship Christ our God

Christ Himself speaks in a text provided for Mattins on Holy Thursday and says this:

> Before the ages the Father begat Me, who am Wisdom and Creator, and He established Me as the beginning of His ways. He appointed me to perform the works which are now mystically accomplished. For though I am by nature the uncreated Word, I make My own the speech and qualities of the manhood that I have assumed.

This is not a quotation from the Gospels; this is a specially written liturgical text. It is completely consistent with the Orthodox doctrine that it enunciates. It is unusual only in that it appears it is Jesus Christ speaking the words and this is not a very frequent occurrence in the liturgy. The Second Person of the Holy Trinity is called the Son. He is not called this because of His birth from Mary, the bearer of God, the Theotokos, but because He is begotten by the Father from the beginning, before the ages, for, as the Nicene Creed declares, we believe:

> in one Lord, Jesus Christ, the only-begotten Son of God, *begotten from the Father before all ages*, Light from Light, true God from true God, begotten not made, consubstantial with the Father, through him all things were made. For our sake and for our salvation he came down from heaven, and was incarnate from the Holy Spirit and the Virgin Mary and became man.

The *Pentecostarion* declares of Christ, 'Thy birth from the Father is timeless and from everlasting', and it adds, 'Thine incarnation of the Virgin is inexpressible and inexplicable to men.'

We are again on the boundaries of language with a need to repeat the same thing in many different ways and again and again, something at which the Orthodox liturgy excels. Always reaffirming the Unity of the Son with the Father and the Holy Spirit, the liturgical texts extol those things done by the Son that manifest God's love for humankind. Orthodoxy stresses the saving purpose of the Incarnation. At Christmas – more correctly called the Feast of the Nativity *after the flesh*, to distinguish it from the birth of the Son, which is without beginning – the liturgy says:

> for behold, the Son and Word of God the Father comes forth to be born of a Maiden who has not known man, by the good pleasure of the Father who begat Him impassibly, and by the co-operation of the Holy Spirit.

Contrast and paradox are stressed again; the Creator makes Himself to be created and, though He fills all things, He is contained within a cave and in a manger.

We see the paradox repeated in texts concerning the death and burial of Christ, such as this one used during the preparation of the gifts in the Liturgy:

> With your body, O Christ, you were in the tomb, with your soul in Hades as God, in Paradise with the Thief, on the throne with Father and Spirit, filling all things, yet yourself uncircumscribed.

The Incarnation of the Son is described in the liturgy in a number of ways: as assuming human nature, being clothed in our substance or in created flesh, being made flesh as man, bearing the form of Adam, the first man, or the likeness of the flesh of Adam, even taking 'the form of a creature of vile clay'. The language of 'being clothed' and the flesh being 'as a garment' is purely figurative. It doesn't mean that Christ only *appeared* to be human, putting on flesh like a robe, for that would be to deny He took flesh from the Virgin Mary. The liturgy stresses the paradox by calling it 'a strange birth'. It can be said of and to Mary that she is the Mother of God, for she is addressed in the liturgy as 'thou [who] hast given birth to

One of the undivided Trinity, thy Son and God'. Again, the liturgy says, 'What mysteries beyond mind and speech!' Nonetheless, and no matter if the thought is confused and the language strained, the Church finds words with which to praise God for these wonders.

St Basil the Great says that God is now on earth, not as a law-giver, with fire and trumpet blast, smoke-wreathed mountain, dense cloud and terrifying storm, as found in Exodus, but 'as one gently and kindly conversing in a human body'. God, he says, is in the flesh:

> He is bringing back to himself the whole human race, which he has taken possession of and united to himself. By his flesh he has made the human race his own kin. But how can glory come to all through only one? How can the Godhead be in the flesh? In the same way as fire can be in iron: not by moving from place to place but by the one imparting to the other its own properties. Fire does not speed toward iron to share its own natural attributes. The fire is not diminished and yet it completely fills whatever shares its nature. So it is also with God the Word. He did not relinquish his own nature and yet he dwelt among us. He did not undergo any change and yet the Word became flesh. Earth received him from heaven, yet heaven was not deserted by him who holds the universe in being.

A Christmas text in the *Festal Menaion* maps the process. Humanity fell from the divine and better life. Though made in the image of God, it became, through transgression, wholly subject to corruption and decay. The wise Creator, seeing that humanity, whom He made with His own hands, was perishing, fashioned us anew. He bowed the heavens and came down, took human substance from the Virgin and was made truly flesh. He was made man and so has won us back again. Because of this, the Church rejoices. Read in isolation, the Christmas texts might suggest that the Incarnation by itself achieves salvation and the redemption of the creation. Instead, the texts declare that, by assuming human nature, God has

13

bestowed on it immortality and salvation: a strange rebirth is granted to those sprung of Adam, the curse that came from the virgin
Eve is removed by the cooperation of the Virgin Mary, the ancient
bond of condemnation is loosed, Paradise is opened, the serpent
is laid low. God has come on earth and man gone up to heaven.
A sticheron attributed to Germanos I, Patriarch of Constantinople
(715–730) and used on 25 December expresses the reasons for joy:

> Come, let us greatly rejoice in the Lord as we tell of this present
> mystery. The middle wall of partition has been destroyed; the
> flaming sword turns back, the cherubim withdraw from the
> tree of life, and I partake of the delight of Paradise from which
> I was cast out through disobedience. For the express Image
> of the Father, the Imprint of His eternity, takes the form of a
> servant, and without undergoing change He comes forth from
> a Mother who knew not wedlock. For what He was, He has
> remained, true God: and what He was not, He has taken upon
> Himself, becoming man through love of mankind. Unto Him
> let us cry aloud: God born of a Virgin, have mercy upon us.

The Nativity is only the beginning. In the symbolic interpretation of the Holy Liturgy and the unfolding events of the liturgical
year, the Person, power and redeeming work of Christ is revealed.
Explaining the Liturgy's symbolic function, Nicholas Cabasilas
notes that it is all connected to the work of redemption and, for
those who already have faith, 'it preserves, renews and increases
what already exists; it makes the believers stronger in faith and
more generous in devotion and love'. It is not a simple picture that is
offered, as to a child, but an idea and a feeling deeply impressed on
the faithful, for Christ is not an abstract doctrine but the one who
sanctifies and the principal place of sanctification is the Liturgy,
which keeps the memory of Christ fresh and leads the faithful from
glory to glory. Hence, the Liturgy rejoices in every aspect of Christ's
ministry but especially in His Nativity and Theophany/Epiphany,
His Transfiguration, His Passion and His Resurrection. Each feast
and commemoration presents Christ not by a simple picture but

by providing a story, interpretation and application. We are told of how Christ healed or raised someone from the dead, the interaction of His divinity and humanity is expounded, and then the appropriate response, in praise and thanksgiving and increase in virtue, is elicited. Everything that Christ does is concerned with salvation. He speaks in the Mattins of Holy Thursday, in words following those quoted above:

> Since I am man not merely in appearance but in reality, the human nature united to Me is made godlike through the exchange of attributes. Know Me, then, as one single Christ, who saves those among whom I have been born and whose nature I have taken.

In this way, the Incarnation and the Passion are so linked together that they are actually inseparable in liturgy, theology, spirituality and in divine and human reality. Orthodoxy would say that this inseparability is nothing new; it is the faith of the Apostles who knew Christ in the flesh and confessed Him as God, who saw His wonders and the manifestation of His glory, and witnessed and proclaimed His death and Resurrection. Certain types of theological reflection, applying the analytical principle and failing to respect the unity of the whole, have divided, dissected and separated the parts. It is against this that the Orthodox faith protests.

A similar unity – that is to say, an inseparability – belongs to Christ's Passion and Resurrection, but it is a wider unity that connects creation, the angelic realm, Christ's baptism and Adam's liberation, the Church, the Virgin Mother and the Resurrection. At the Service of the Twelve Gospels on Holy Friday (usually Holy Thursday night), when in Greek churches the cross from the sanctuary is carried into the centre of the church, the choir sings this antiphon:

> Today He who hung the earth upon the waters is hung upon the Cross (*three times*).
> He who is King of the angels is arrayed in a crown of thorns.

He who wraps the heaven in clouds is wrapped in the purple
of mockery.
He who in Jordan set Adam free receives blows upon His face.
The Bridegroom of the Church is pierced with a spear.
The Son of the Virgin is pierced with a spear.
We venerate Thy Passion, O Christ (*three times*).
Show us also Thy glorious Resurrection.

There is sometimes a sense that those who wrote and compiled liturgical texts didn't know when to stop. That is because they were
powerfully aware of the theological unity and the way in which
themes converge and co-penetrate. Dogmatic theology and liturgy
are not two separate matters or two separate studies. As Sergei
Bulgakov taught, dogma is not a freestanding philosophical system
but rooted in the prayer of the Church, both the personal prayer of
Christians and the liturgical prayer of the community. The type of
theology is less important than the type of theologian. An Orthodox
would not understand how the German-American scholar Paul
Tillich could be a theologian when he had to be reminded by the
Dean of Union Theological Seminary that the faculty went to chapel
services. Bulgakov said that the altar and the theologian's cell – the
theologian's workplace – must be conjoined. As he expressed it, 'the
deepest origins of the theologian's inspiration must be nourished
from the altar'. This is what we might call 'liturgical knowing' that
comes through participation in a worshipping community standing before God in prayer. It is John of Damascus, equally at home as
a liturgical poet and as a dogmatic theologian, sitting at his desk or
standing in church, who summarizes so well the saving work that
restores to humankind what was lost:

Well done, O Christ, O Wisdom and Power and Word of God,
and God almighty! What should we resourceless people give
Thee in return for all things? For all things are Thine and Thou
askest nothing of us but that we be saved. Even this Thou hast
given us, and by Thy ineffable goodness Thou art grateful
to those who accept it. Thanks be to Thee who hast given

being and the grace of well-being and who by Thy ineffable condescension hast brought back to this state those who fell from it.

(*The Orthodox Faith*, Book 4, Chapter 5)

O Heavenly King, Comforter, Spirit of Truth

The morning prayer that begins with these words and continues 'who art everywhere present and fillest all things, Treasury of good things and Giver of life' is the one that is most frequently repeated in Orthodoxy. It is the most basic and essential invocation of the Holy Spirit, the Third Person of the Holy Trinity, and urges the Spirit to 'come and dwell in us, and cleanse us from all impurity, and save our souls, O Good One'. In the Orthodox Church, there is a doctrine of the Holy Spirit and there is, more importantly, an experience of the Holy Spirit. In his *Catechetical Lectures*, Cyril of Jerusalem wants the catechumens to have a grasp of the doctrine, but what he really wants is that those who are to be baptized should be sealed with the Spirit and receive the Spirit's gifts. This is part of what he teaches as he addresses the clause in the baptismal creed of Jerusalem that says, 'and in one Holy Spirit, the Paraclete, who spake by the prophets'.

He it is who through the prophets predicted the things of Christ, he again who worked mightily in the apostles. To this day it is he who in the sacrament seals the souls of those who are baptized. These are all gifts of the Father to the Son, who imparts them to the Holy Spirit. That is not my saying, but Jesus himself says, 'All things are delivered unto me of my Father' (Matt. 11.27); while, of the Holy Spirit he says, 'When he, the Spirit of truth shall come . . .' and so on, ending, 'he shall glorify me; for he shall receive of mine, and shall show it unto you' (John 16.13, 14). Every grace is given by the Father, through the Son, who also acts together with the Holy Spirit.

There are not some graces that come from the Father, and different graces from the Son, and others again from the Holy Spirit. There is but one salvation, one giving of power, one faith, and yet there is one God the Father, our Lord, his only-begotten Son, and one Holy Spirit, the Paraclete. Let us be content with this knowledge and not busy ourselves with questions about the divine nature or hypostasis. I would have spoken of that had it been contained in Scriptures. Let us not venture where Scripture does not lead, for it suffices for our salvation to know that there is Father, and Son, and Holy Spirit. (*Catechetical Lectures*, XVI, 24)

Though John of Damascus is quite at home discussing the divine nature and hypostasis, he can also provide a concise summary of doctrine based on Scripture that surely would have satisfied Cyril:

The Son is the image of the Father and the image of the Son is the Spirit, through whom Christ dwelling in man gives it to him to be also the image of God.

The Holy Ghost is God. He is the median of the Unbegotten and the Begotten and He is joined with the Father through the Son. He is called Spirit of God, Spirit of Christ, Mind of Christ, Spirit of the Lord, True Lord, Spirit of adoption, freedom, and wisdom – for He is the cause of all things. He fills all things with His essence and sustains all things. In His essence He fills the world, but in His power the world does not contain Him. (*The Orthodox Faith*, Book 1, Chapter 13)

The liturgy says less about the Person and nature of the Holy Spirit than it does about the effects of the Spirit, as when the priest at the Eucharist asks, 'enable me by the power of thy Holy Spirit' or standing at the Holy Table prays, 'Send down Thy Holy Spirit upon us and upon these Gifts set forth'.

As might be expected, it is in spiritual and ascetical writing and practice that the greatest attention is paid to the Holy Spirit. In the sayings of the Desert Fathers we hear of an Abba from Rome who is described as 'a man full of discernment and the good odour of the Holy Spirit' and, by Abba Daniel, in the words of Acts 11.24 as 'filled with the Holy Spirit and faith'. This is almost certainly Arsenius, a Roman of senatorial rank, employed by Emperor Theodosius I, who left the palace in his mid-thirties and became a desert anchorite in Egypt. Abba John the Dwarf teaches that when the Holy Spirit descends into human hearts, they are renewed and, like palm trees after abundant rain, put forth leaves in the fear of God. The opposite of this growth is described by Abba Orosius as the consequence of neglect of spiritual matters. He says it is like a lamp filled with oil and lit. If we forget to replenish the oil, gradually it goes out and darkness will prevail. In the same way, through the soul's negligence, the Holy Spirit gradually withdraws until its warmth is completely extinguished. This practical understanding of the Spirit passed through Palestine and Syria to Kiev and into the heart of Russian spirituality. N. A. Motivilov, a disciple of St Seraphim of Sarov, had a conversation with the great staretz on a grey winter day, when a few inches of snow lay on the ground and a rather heavy sleet was falling. Motivilov was seated on the stump of a newly felled tree and Father Seraphim squatted before him. In such unlikely circumstances they talked of the Holy Spirit. Guiding him towards the true goal of the Christian life, Father Seraphim said:

> Therefore, God-loving one, it is in the acquisition of this Spirit of God that the true goal of our Christian life consists: whereas prayer, watching, fasting, alms and other virtuous practices engaged in for Christ's sake are only the means of acquiring the Spirit of God.

St Seraphim used the analogy of trade. What is important for the Christian is to build up capital, an eternal capital of grace. Life is like a marketplace and the task is to trade, using good deeds, virtuous actions and prayer, though these only accumulate profit when undertaken for Christ's sake. He explains that, at baptism, we receive the precious gifts of the Holy Spirit, which would be sufficient for us if we did not squander them through sin and corruption. This decline can be reversed if we are awakened by the divine wisdom that seeks our salvation. The elder continues:

In spite of our sinfulness, in spite of the darkness surrounding our souls, the Grace of the Holy Spirit, conferred by Baptism in the name of the Father, the Son and the Holy Spirit, still shines in our heart with the inextinguishable light of Christ's priceless merits. And when the sinner turns to the way of repentance, this light smooths away every trace of the sins committed, clothing the former sinner in the garments of incorruption, spun of the Grace of the Holy Spirit. It is of the acquisition of this Grace, as of the goal of the Christian life, that I have been speaking all this time, God-loving one.

Theologian Vladimir Lossky described the words of St Seraphim as a definition that sums up the whole spiritual tradition of the Orthodox Church.

In this way, the Holy Trinity is the foundation, purpose and fulfilment of the Orthodox Christian faith. Just as St Seraphim could not speak of the Holy Spirit without also speaking of Christ the Son and of God the Father, so all of Orthodox theology, liturgy and spirituality is marked by, and constantly refers to, the Holy Trinity, moving always between the One and the Three.

An Orthodox life begins with baptism in the name of the Father and of the Son and of the Holy Spirit – a rite that defines a boundary and puts the baptized on the right side of it. The initial petitions of the rite are clear in asking that the name of the one being received into the Church by baptism is to be inserted in the Book of Life and the Holy Trinity is to be glorified in this person. The second part of the rite involves the banishing of the Devil by the power of God. The candidate for baptism is removed from the domain, power and influence of the Devil and is placed in a constant relationship, described as a yoking, to a radiant guardian angel, 'who shall deliver him/her from every snare of the adversary, from encounter with evil, from the demon of the noonday, and from evil visions'. The spirits of guile, idolatry and every concupiscence, the spirit of deceit and every uncleanness are expelled, and the one to be baptized is called 'a reason-endowed sheep in the holy flock of Christ, an honourable member of the Church, a consecrated vessel, a child of light, an heir of the Kingdom'. Satan is renounced and literally spat on. The one being baptized is united to Christ, puts off the old self and is 'no more a child of the body, but a child of [the] Kingdom'. The victory over evil is brought to its fullness in the blessing of the water – water being the primal element of the material world. Anointed, baptized by triple immersion and clothed 'with the robe of righteousness', the newly baptized is Chrismated by being anointed six times with the holy Chrism, each time with the words, 'The seal of the gift of the Holy Spirit'. The cutting of hair – the last rite of the baptismal liturgy – is a sign that human life is itself transformed into service, into liturgy, into the work of Christ. The full meaning of what is done is contained in the Epistle read at baptism from St Paul's letter to the Romans (6.3–11) that begins 'Do you not know that all of us who have been baptized into Christ Jesus were baptized into his death?' (NRSV). The same understanding is expressed in Eastertide by the oft-repeated chant, taken from Galatians 3.27: 'As many of you as were baptized into Christ, have put on Christ.' To live as an Orthodox is to live as a conscious citizen of the Kingdom that is and is to come, and for that very reason the great central act of Orthodoxy, the Holy Liturgy, begins with a Trinitarian affirmation that also unites the present age to one to come: 'Blessed is the Kingdom of the Father, and of the Son, and of the Holy Spirit, now and for ever, and to the ages of ages. Amen.'

2

The Orthodox ethos

'My hope is the Father, my refuge the Son, my shelter the Holy Spirit. O Holy Trinity, glory be to Thee.' This is a concise statement of the personal faith of an Orthodox Christian. It is a practical statement of belief and attitude, attributed to St Joannicius the Great (*c.* 740–834), rather than a fully elaborated theological statement. It says nothing, for example, about the Church, the liturgy and the sacraments. Even a full statement cannot explain the spirit or ethos of Orthodoxy – that is to say, the distinctive features which give it the character, flavour and texture that go beyond the faith expressed in the first chapter and make it recognizable as what it is. There are at least five such features, which might be labelled beauty, boundaries, asceticism, biography and miracle.

Beauty

The beauty that defines Orthodoxy is divine. The Deity, as St Gregory of Nyssa teaches, is in very substance Beautiful. The purified soul will always be drawn to this Beauty. Purified from every vice it will be and remain in this sphere of Beauty. The real assimilation of the divine is to be found in making our own life in some degree a copy of the Supreme Being. The Beautiful is necessarily lovable. Unlike earthly desire, where the beautiful is seen as something to possess and where possession leads to satiety, nothing interrupts the capacity to love the Beautiful. The Christian finds within the Church and its mysteries the anticipation of the vision of that Beauty, so wishes to be like that which is as yet perceived as through a mirror, dimly or darkly. What unfolds in worship leads Christians to the discovery that they can be changed into something better than themselves. The Scriptures teach them this, the sacraments teach them this, the icons present the transformed image of what humans can be through the experience of the divine Beauty. There can only be true delight in the fitting structure of the church building, its furnishings and decoration, its icons and music, if those who have put on Christ become, by grace and by effort, Christlike. St Gregory ventures to affirm that, to one who has cleansed all the powers of his or her being from every form of vice, the Beauty that is essential, the source of every beauty and every good, will become visible. That confidence is a feature of Orthodoxy. The memory of this Beauty is never lost to the Church but is preserved, even if not always in its freshest and most vigorous form, so that as, by the prompting of the Holy Spirit, the desire is again nourished, the Church herself acknowledges that this is what she should be, the Bride of the Lamb, robed in glory for the Bridegroom. Beauty in Orthodoxy is not an aesthetic preference but a necessary intimation of the divine. Nonetheless, it manifests itself in all those ways in which inexhaustible divine Beauty can be present, in all parts of the Church and her members.

In his well-known book *The Confessions*, Augustine of Hippo points to the result of harmonious combination when he says that 'a thing which consists of several parts, each beautiful in itself, is far more beautiful than the individual parts which, properly combined and arranged, compose the whole, even though each part, taken separately, is itself a thing of beauty'. The Orthodox Church combines parts that are beautiful in themselves into a whole that is yet more beautiful, and this is most clearly demonstrated by the Liturgy. We can say that it combines pleasing architectural forms, ornament and decoration with ceremonial and musical beauty. We can also say that, in icons, prose, poetry, singing and ritual, it beautifully combines purity of doctrine and a steadfast desire for God into a translucent whole. The nature of these combinations has been described as heaven on earth. John Chrysostom, in the fourth century, said that 'the church is a place of the angels, of the archangels, the kingdom of God, heaven itself'. In the same way the eighth-century commentator on the Liturgy, Germanos of

Constantinople, said that 'the church is an earthly heaven in which the heavenly God dwells and moves'. According to the Russian Primary Chronicle, written by Nestor the Chronicler, a monk of the Kiev Pechersky (Caves) monastery, the envoys of Prince Vladimir, who had been to a mosque in Bulgaria and a church in Germany, reported in this way after attending the Liturgy at the Great Church, the Hagia Sophia, in Constantinople:

> Then we went on to Greece, and the Greeks led us to the edifices where they worship their God, and we knew not whether we were in heaven or on earth. For on earth there is no such splendour or such beauty, and we are at a loss how to describe it. We know only that God dwells there among men, and their service is fairer than the ceremonies of other nations. For we cannot forget that beauty.

Among the *obiter dicta* of American art historian and authority on Byzantine architecture Robert Ousterhout is the claim that it was on the basis of architecture that Russia accepted Orthodoxy. More accurately, the Russian historian and linguist Dmitry Likhachev wrote that beauty determined the nature of Orthodoxy in Russia and that it was 'beauty beyond intellectual justifications [that] allowed the content of church doctrine and its sanctity to be preserved'. It was a beauty that derived from Byzantium, which developed with its own distinctive Russian style. The church building, no matter how humble or grand it may be, and the Liturgy celebrated within it, express this beauty, not as something to be looked at or listened to, like the beauty found in art gallery and theatre, but as something in which the faithful are fully participant as an integral part of the whole.

Boundaries

'Name?' asked the priest rather curtly as someone not known to him presented themselves to receive communion in a local Orthodox church. He wanted to know because communion is always administered by name, the priest declaring, 'The servant of God *N.* partakes of the precious and holy Body and Blood of our Lord and God and Saviour Jesus Christ unto the remission of sins and unto eternal life.' The next question was, 'Are you baptized Orthodox?' And then it might be, 'Have you been to confession? Have you fasted?' The Orthodox seem ready for the questioning and are hardly ever put out by it or terribly upset when turned away. They know the rules. The rules maintain a boundary line, keeping out those not qualified to receive communion and ensuring that the faithful Orthodox, duly prepared, can. A person seeking to include names among the prayers at the Liturgy in a Russian church may find a notice that declares, 'the unbaptized, people of other faiths, unbelievers and suicides are not commemorated in the church'. It is another example of a clear boundary. Such a boundary separates the Orthodox Christian from unbelievers and from others who claim to be Christian, but aren't (by Orthodox standards), and there are less definite, even rather fuzzy, boundaries encountered by those who move between the various Orthodox churches and communities. Some of these boundaries and the reasons for them are to do with language, some with ethnicity, some with the calendar, some with differences in spiritual practice and discipline, particularly with regard to confession and frequency of communion, and some arise from less specific cultural differences. There are also the boundaries created by different and competing jurisdictions, such as those of the Ecumenical Patriarch of Constantinople (Istanbul) and the Patriarch of Moscow.

The first significant boundary to take notice of is that between Christians and non-Christians, which is felt most strongly where the Orthodox Church has been persecuted. Orthodoxy was born in the Roman Empire and the Church's first saints are martyrs who refused to deny their faith in Jesus Christ and to worship the pagan gods. Many of these were lay people and various examples can be drawn from the calendar of saints. In September alone, we can find the Holy Martyrs Menodora, Metrodora and Nymphodora, commemorated on the tenth, and the Holy Great Martyr Eustathius and his family, commemorated on the twentieth. The first group were sisters who lived in virginity and devoted themselves to asceticism and prayer. Someone betrayed them and, refusing to deny Christ, they were tortured and killed in the reign of the Emperor Maximian in 304. Eustathius, before baptism, was called Placidas and he was a Roman general in the days of the Emperor Trajan. He, his wife Theopiste and their two sons, Agapius and Theopistus, became Christians and were then persecuted. All their goods were stolen and they became separated from one another on a pilgrimage to Jerusalem. Reunited after many years, they returned to Rome, but Eustathius refused to sacrifice to the idols, and he and his family were martyred in 126 under the Emperor Hadrian.

The calendar abounds with such early martyrs. Their stories in the *Menaion* are generally familiar to the Orthodox faithful and provide a model for response to persecution by non-Christians. Orthodox churches suffered persecution after the Muslim conquest of formerly Christian lands and during Ottoman rule. From this period there are a number of 'new martyrs' (neo-martyrs), called this to differentiate them from the martyrs of the Early Church, including Muslims who converted to Christianity and were killed. The Orthodox also suffered persecution in the twentieth century in atheistic communist states, in the Soviet Union and its satellites, and there are a significant group of new martyrs and confessors from that period. There are also a group of new martyrs of Serbia from the Second World War and the Nazi occupation.

The second significant boundary is between the Orthodox and heretics. The Greek word *hairesis* literally means 'choice'. When the Jewish writer Josephus affirmed that 'Jewish doctrine takes three forms' he used the word *hairesis* to mean 'doctrinal school', and the three he mentioned (two of which are known to us from the New Testament) were Pharisees, Sadducees and Essenes. For Christians it meant not just choice, or the choosing of one doctrinal approach from others, but 'wrong choice'. A heresy was an error, a teaching that opposed some essential part of the Christian faith. John of Damascus, in one of his last works, *The Fount of Knowledge*, written after 743, lists and briefly describes 103 heresies, ending with what he calls 'the superstition of the Ishmaelites which to this day prevails and keeps people in error, being a forerunner of the Antichrist'; this is Islam. Certain heresies have left a deep impression on Orthodoxy; among them are Arianism, Nestorianism and the Iconoclastic heresy. Arianism, so-called after its author, Arius (d. *c.* 336), denied the true divinity of Jesus Christ and was opposed by numerous Fathers and most notably by Athanasius, Hilary of Poitiers and the Cappadocian Fathers, Basil, Gregory of Nazianzus and Gregory of Nyssa. It was finally condemned at the Council of Constantinople in 381. Nestorianism, which takes its name from Nestorius (d. *c.* 451), held that there were two separate Persons in Christ, one divine, the other human, against the Orthodox doctrine of the Incarnate Christ as a single Person, at once God and man. It also rejected the title Theotokos ('God-bearer') applied to the Blessed Virgin Mary. The leading opponent was Cyril of Alexandria and Nestorius's teaching was condemned at the Council of Ephesus in 431. The controversy over the veneration of icons raged from *c.* 725 until 842, beginning with the Emperor Leo the Isaurian (717– 741), who held that the excessive veneration of icons was the chief obstacle to the conversion of Jews and Muslims. This was not just a theological argument. During this period churches were despoiled, icons destroyed and the defenders of icons persecuted. After a period of restoration of icons at the end of the eighth and into the next century, there was a second period of iconoclastic persecution from 814 until 842. Some historians of Byzantium have advanced what might be called a revisionist approach to iconoclasm, but the Church puts the witness of its martyrs before even the well-intentioned speculation of scholars. The first Sunday of Great Lent is a celebration in honour of icons, known as the Feast of Orthodoxy.

The language applied to the defenders of Orthodoxy in the liturgy is significant. Athanasius is called 'Orthodoxy's steadfast pillar' and Hilary of Poitiers the 'defender of Orthodoxy and right belief'. Athanasius and Cyril of Alexandria are described as those who 'quenched every false belief and teaching'. Cyril and a number of other Fathers are each acclaimed as 'Guide of Orthodoxy, teacher of piety and holiness, luminary of the world, God-inspired adornment of hierarchs'. By contrast the liturgy speaks of 'impious heretics' and 'the wolves of error' together with the 'dark despondency of heresy' and the 'webs of heresies'. Those who opposed heresy are champions, leaders, defenders of right belief, teachers, unshakeable pillars, true keepers and guardians of apostolic traditions, sure and brilliant exponents of Orthodoxy. The same language is applied to St Mark Eugenicus, Metropolitan of Ephesus (d. 1443), who refused to sign the decree of unity between Rome and the Orthodox of the Council of Florence, and to St Tikhon, the Patriarch of Moscow (d. 1925), 'a confessor under the atheist yoke'. The preaching of the Apostles and the doctrines of the Fathers confirm the one faith of the Church, and the Church wears 'the garment of truth woven from theology on high', also referred to as 'the robe of Orthodoxy woven in heaven'. Heresy is an error that is internal to the Church, an assault on its beliefs and a rending of the fabric. It divides families, friends and communities, impairs communion and damages the Church's witness. The experience of heresy, like the experience of persecution, marks the Church. Without going as far as accusing everyone with whom one cannot agree of heresy, which often happens in Orthodox social media posts, boundary maintenance is a truly important part of the Orthodox mentality. It must be clear what Orthodoxy is and the Orthodox tradition must be maintained. It must not be substantially altered, diluted or diminished.

The third significant boundary is really a consequence of the second; it is the boundary between Orthodoxy and all other bodies that claim to be Christian churches. Some of the specific differences are identified in the usual form for the reception of converts. A convert entering the Orthodox Church from some other confession is required to renounce all errors and false doctrines and mistakes of judgement and all ancient and modern heresies, and then to confess the Orthodox faith. Different confessions, Roman–Latin (Roman Catholic), Armenian, Lutheran and Reformed, have different sets of questions, though there is not a set specific to the Anglican–Episcopal confession. For the Armenians it is a question of the two natures in Christ. For the Roman Catholics and the churches of the Reformation it is first a renunciation of the words of the Filioque ('and the Son') in the description of the Procession

of the Holy Spirit, and then specific questions relevant to each confession about papal primacy and infallibility, predestination, the
eucharistic transformation of bread and wine into the Body and
Blood of Christ, the number of the sacraments, reverence for the
saints and prayer for the dead. Modern heresies are, however, rather
different from historic heresies. Metropolitan Alfeyev, explaining the continued participation of the Russian Orthodox Church
in the World Council of Churches, pointed to the difference between the churches that value and uphold tradition, including
traditional moral values (the Orthodox, the Roman Catholics and
the churches known as Pre-Chalcedonian) and those that espouse
what are generally called liberal doctrines and values. These are
mostly Protestant churches, though some Protestants, especially in
Africa, hold to traditional moral values. The Metropolitan, head of
External Affairs for the Moscow Patriarchate, takes quite a prag-
matic approach to participation in ecumenical bodies while holding
that only traditional bodies can effectively oppose militant liber-
alism, militant atheism and militant Islam. The maintenance of
boundaries is not an activity essentially opposed to dialogue, but
one that promotes honesty within the dialogue.

The fourth boundary, weaker than the others yet still present, is
between jurisdictions, ethnicities and languages. If a person says, 'I
am Orthodox', then the next question is likely to be, 'Are you Greek
or Russian?' One perfectly serious reply to that is that it is irrelevant;
Orthodox is Orthodox is Orthodox. There is only one Orthodox
Church and it is the One, Holy, Catholic, and Apostolic Church of
the Nicene Creed. Every member of the Church knows that the words
said at the Great Entrance that ask God to remember in His Kingdom
'all of you Orthodox Christians' apply equally to them and to all
others who hold the Orthodox Christian faith. As the Trinity combines the many and the one, so too there are many churches, but only
one Orthodox Church. A joint statement by the Patriarch of Serbia
and the Patriarch of Antioch, issued in October 2018, affirmed that

the Orthodox Church is one, holy, catholic and apostolic,
and is not a federation or a confederation of churches that are

separate and independent from each other, acting and reacting based on self-interests, and which appear to the world as a group of Churches in conflict, in dispute, and in estrangement between each other.

It is still necessary to acknowledge that there is difference, even if it falls short of division, within this one Church. Some of the differences are the product of history. Orthodox history is necessarily tied up with the history of the Roman Empire, of Byzantium and of the conflict with Islam. In the eleventh century, as we have seen, Christianity was embraced by ancient Russia and so was caught up in Russian history too. Texts in Slavonic came by way of Bulgaria and bishops came initially from the Greek world, but something distinctively Russian soon developed in terms of language, liturgy, monasticism and spirituality. The pattern is repeated across the world of Eastern European Orthodoxy. The historical and ethnic divisions are exported through the Orthodox diaspora to other countries in the same way that Western European religious history and division was exported across the world in the colonial period.

Since 2009, a Pan-Orthodox Episcopal Assembly has existed in a number of countries that have multiple Orthodox communities in order to promote unity and cohesion. There is one in the British Isles made up of all the active, canonical Orthodox bishops with churches in Britain and Ireland. Its members are identified by the jurisdiction to which they belong rather than to the Russian Orthodox Church, Greek Orthodox Church and so on. Its ability to function depends on the maintenance of communion between the jurisdictions, so that pan-Orthodox relations were interrupted by the disputes between Constantinople and Rome over Estonia in the 1990s and over the Ukraine in 2018–2019. The current membership would represent the Ecumenical Patriarchate of Constantinople, the Moscow Patriarchate, the Patriarchates of Serbia, Romania, Bulgaria and Georgia, the Russian Orthodox Church Outside Russia (ROCOR), the Ukrainian Exarchate of the Ecumenical Patriarchate, the Patriarchate of Antioch (in Syria) and all the East, and the Exarchate of Parishes of the Russian Tradition in Western

Europe (Ecumenical Patriarchate, suppressed late in 2018, but not yet abolished in 2019).

The various titles reveal some of the history of Orthodoxy in Western Europe. The long-established Greek Orthodox Church comes under the Ecumenical Patriarchate in the British Diocese of Thyateira. As a result of British history in the Mediterranean, many parishes have a predominance of Greek Cypriots. There are three Russian jurisdictions. They are the Moscow Patriarchate Diocese of Sourozh, with its clear links to Moscow, ROCOR and the Exarchate of Russian Tradition Parishes, under the Ecumenical Patriarch. ROCOR, formerly ROCA (Russian Orthodox Church Abroad) was a temporary expedient begun in the 1920s as a response to the Russian Revolution. Initially it was the church of Russian refugees. It maintained links with the patriarchate while resisting the influence on the church of the Soviet authorities. After many years of negotiation ROCOR and the Moscow Patriarchate were reconciled and entered full communion in 2007. ROCOR has Holy Trinity monastery and seminary in Jordanville, New York, and their liturgical publications are very popular. In 1927 the parishes governed by Metropolitan Evlogy Georgievsky parted company with ROCOR and in due course became an Exarchate under the Ecumenical Patriarch in 1931. It is particularly associated with its cathedral in the rue Daru in Paris and with the Saint-Sergius Orthodox Theological Institute, founded by Evlogy in 1925, though he himself returned to the Moscow Patriarchate towards the end of his life. The other members of the Pan-Orthodox Assembly represent ethnically specific groups of Orthodox Christians who have migrated to Britain at various times. The version of the Liturgy of St John Chrysostom used in Sourozh Diocese includes, in the Litany of Fervent Supplication, a welcome prayer for 'this country, and for all our countries and their peoples, whether dwelling therein or now scattered abroad'.

Asceticism

The elders-anchorites and ever-sinless
maidens,

To fly with their right heart to the precincts
    of Heavens,
To make it strong enough in earthly storms
    and fight,
Composed many prayers to recite.
But not a single prayer for me is so dear
As one which from a priest we're often
    blessed to hear
In so mournful, so solemn days of Lent.
This prayer very oft on lips of mine is set,
And fallen me provides with strengths I'd
    never known:
Oh, Lord of all my days! The ghost of idle-
    ness low
And sensuality – this cunning snake and
    hard –
And empty talk – don't pass into my heart.
But help me, Lord, to see my own sins'
    procession,
Let ne'er brother of mine receive my
    condemnation,
And let the air of patience, meekness, love
And blessed chastity in my heart turn alive.
(Pushkin, 1836; translated by Yevgeny Bonver,
2003; altered)

Pushkin, in this late poem written in the year prior to his death, is summarizing the prayer that has been described as a favourite of the Russian people, the prayer of St Ephraim the Syrian used on every weekday throughout Great Lent.

O Lord and Master of my life, a spirit of idleness, despondency, ambition and idle talking give me not. *Prostration.*
But rather a spirit of chastity, humble-mindedness, patience, and love bestow upon me Thy servant. *Prostration.*
Yea, O Lord King, grant me to see my failings and not to

condemn my brother; for blessed art Thou unto the ages of ages. Amen. *Prostration.*

This prayer expresses the moral qualities and virtues that are characteristic of Orthodox saints. Reinforced by frequent repetition of the prayer, these qualities become part of what it means to be a Christian in the annual ascetic combat of Lent, the arena in which, like the martyrs of old, Christians challenge all that would detach them from obedience to Christ. Asceticism is, in that sense, a contest and spectacle. The spiritual within contests the primacy of the material. Fasting is an essential element in this ascetic contest. It is said of the founders of the Russian monastery of Valaam in Lake Ladoga, Saints Sergius and Herman, that they wisely subjected their bodies to the spirit by fasts, vigils and by standing all night, presumably in prayer. In the *Paterikon* of the Kiev Pechersky monastery we can find multiple examples of those who practised what we might consider rather extreme asceticism through silence, seclusion, self-restraint, fasting, obedience, bodily suffering, non-acquisitiveness and voluntary poverty. Those who took a less demanding approach were also constant in their labours, avoiding all idleness. This ascetic tradition goes back to the Fathers and Mothers of the Egyptian desert, of Syria and of the Holy Land, hermits, anchorites and stylites, and especially to St Anthony the Great. It flowered also in the community-based monasteries, where monks lived a life in common according to a rule, and, as the faithful sought spiritual guidance from elders and confessors in the monasteries and hermitages, it permeated ordinary Christian life with the risk that it made it look as if salvation was only to be achieved by abandoning this world for the monastic life. Asceticism of this sort is often held up, not least by reading the lives of the largely monastic saints, as that to which all Christians should aspire.

St Dimitri of Rostov (1651–1709), one of the most celebrated preachers of the Russian Church, taught that it was the duty of all Christians to strive for unity with God, because God is the centre and final purpose of the soul and it is from God that the soul received its life and nature. Dimitri says that the visible things of the world which are lovable and desirable, everything beautiful, sweet and attractive, belong not to the soul but to the body. As such they are temporary and will pass away, but the soul, being eternal, can only attain rest in the eternal God. God is the soul's highest good, more perfect than all worldly beauty, sweetness and loveliness. In our temporary earthly life we must seek union with God, in order that we may be accounted worthy to be with Him eternally, and this necessarily involves turning away from worldly things. This requires asceticism and it requires prayer. Asceticism is a disciplined letting go of worldly wealth and comfort as part of the striving for God. In that it must be disciplined it requires the sort of constancy and commitment that we might associate with intending to run a marathon or to perform some similar demanding activity. The act of letting go means no longer satisfying every passing whim or desire, every temptation to indulgence, but counting them as of no importance compared with God. Asceticism may bring benefits in terms of health and well-being, but its purpose, if it is to have any spiritual meaning, must be found in the soul's need for God.

The prayer of Ephraim the Syrian is rendered in different ways in English, depending on whether it is translated from Greek or Slavonic. Whatever version is used, the prayer points to a number of common failings and their remedies while stressing above all that Christians should be aware of their own failings rather than those of other people. It is certainly not the case that Orthodox Christians are pinched and dour. They have an inner joy closely connected to realism about themselves and faith in God, who is so often described as philanthropic, a true lover of humankind. They know how to fast and how to feast. If Lent can be austere, and it can be, Easter, the Great Pascha, is always profoundly joyful.

Biography

Orthodoxy has been described somewhere as an oral culture that uses writing. By contrast the churches of the Western European Reformation (from which many converts to Orthodoxy have come) are literate and book-centred. The opposite of 'literate' is not 'illiterate' but 'oral'. This contrast may also be related to one that Likhachev points to – that between the universities as the centres of knowledge in Europe and the monasteries as the centres in Russia at the time of Peter the Great. An oral tradition is a story-telling tradition, and the best stories are those of some person of note. In the Christian tradition that means the acts, words and miracles of the saints and martyrs. Orthodox preaching generally draws on the life and experience of notable believers, and Orthodox theology will often draw on illustrations from the lives, and not just from the teaching, of the Fathers. Many of the books in an Orthodox book-shop or library will be lives of godly women and men. Biography shapes Orthodox life and has done since the story of the death of Polycarp of Smyrna defined the main themes for the lives of the martyrs, and the life of St Anthony of Egypt, written by St Athanasius, established a standard for the lives of saints, especial-ly monastic saints. A collection of lives may be called a paterikon, a book of things concerning the Fathers, that develops into a record to pass on to future generations the lives, wonders and instruc-tions of the Fathers. Such ancient texts include the *Apophthegmata Patrum*, the sayings of the Desert Fathers, Palladius's account of early monasticism in the *Lausiac History* (named from its dedica-tion to an imperial chamberlain, Lausus) and lives of the saints, monks and hermits of Egypt, Syria and the Holy Land, among them lives of St Mary of Egypt and of the harlot Pelagia. In the Slavic tradition, the most important such work is the *Paterikon* of the Kiev Pechersky Lavra, which includes the lives of the found-ers, St Anthony and St Theodosius, their successors as abbots and the huge number of saints of the monastery buried in the caves. It narrates failures as well as successes in the spiritual life, the virtues and the faults of the monks, and has been accurately described as a chronicle of steadfast spiritual endeavour. The *Kiev Paterikon* was completed around 1226 and includes the writings of St Nestor the Chronicler from the late eleventh to early twelfth century. Another example, this time from the sixteenth century, is the *Paterikon* of the monastery of Volokolamsk, some 130 kilometres north-west of Moscow. Later, the lives of individual saints become more frequent, including those of St Tikhon of Zadonsk, St Sergius of Radonezh and St Seraphim of Sarov, all of whom influenced Russian literature.

There are many modern additions to these lives. Popular among them are those of a number of saints and elders associated with Mount Athos: St Porphyrios (1906–1991), St Paisios (1924–1994), Elder Joseph the Hesychast (1897–1959), St Silouan and Elder Sophrony. 'If I were to tell you about my life on the Holy Mountain, my love and my devotion, time would fail me to tell . . . My love for you incites me to tell you what I remember.' These words open the recollections of St Porphyrios of Kafsokalivia concerning his arrival as a twelve-year-old boy on Mount Athos in 1918. Shortly after he arrived, during the first few days, he was woken after midnight by Father Ioannikios who took him to church:

> in three minutes we had arrived at the Holy Trinity church. He ushered me into the church first. It was the first time I had been inside. I was overwhelmed! The church was filled with monks standing upright in an attitude of reverence and attentiveness. The chandeliers shed their light everywhere, lighting up the icons on the walls and on the icon stands. Everything was bright and shining. The little oil lamps were lit, the incense exuded fragrance and the singing resonated devoutly in the otherworldly beauty of the night. I was overcome with awe, but also with fear. I felt that I was no longer on earth, but that I had been transported to heaven. Father Ioannikios nodded to me to go forward and kiss the icons. I remained motionless. 'Take my hand, take my hand!' I gasped. 'I'm scared!' He took me by the hand and, gripping him tightly, I went up to venerate the icons. It was my first experience. It was engraved on my innermost soul. I will never forget it.

The account of Porphyrios's life and teaching was prepared by the Sisters of the Holy Convent of Chrysopigi from materials brought to them by two women who knew the saint for more than thirty years. The Greek text and the excellent English translation preserve the immediacy of his words. They were published in Greek in 2003 and in English, as *Wounded By Love*, in 2005. In 2013 Porphyrios was declared a saint.

The lives, sayings and miracles of the saints have always been important in Orthodoxy and the biographical tradition continues. We can see at once that the life and teachings of St Porphyrios advance two of the strands discussed here. The first, in the passage quoted as well as elsewhere in the book, is the awe-inspiring beauty of Orthodox worship, a beauty that can only be described as other-worldly. The second is the way in which this life presents an immediate experience of monastic life and devotion and encourages an interaction with it, just as the Christians of modern Athens used to search out Porphyrios himself for confession and spiritual guidance. We could add the third strand of godly wisdom that is evident from the beginning, in the sayings of the Desert Fathers. Porphyrios makes much of his simplicity in human terms and the paucity of his education. His is not intellectual asceticism. It is not the wisdom of this world. He lives a life of devotion and trust in a simple and accessible way and his story presents unity with God as a possibility for ordinary people.

Miracle

Miracle is an important aspect of Orthodox faith. There is an expectation that miracles will happen, some in answer to prayer and some, unasked for, as acts of divine providence. Individual miracles must be set against a background of expectation. There are wonder-working icons, weeping icons of the Theotokos, bodies of the saints that remain incorrupt, and myrrh that streams from some of them, as in the case of St Demetrios the Myrrh-streamer (feast day 26 October) and from skulls in the caves of the Kiev Pechersky Lavra. There are places of pilgrimage where healings and other miracles are expected to happen. There are highly venerated relics of the saints. Although miracles are expected, the nature of the miracles is often unexpected. Here are three examples involving dreams or visions.

St Porphyrios broke his leg and various complications with the fracture kept him in bed at the hospital in Athens where he was the chaplain. As he started to walk again, his consultant said that he needed a walking stick. Unable to afford one, he asked his sister to buy one. As she prepared to set out, a woman holding a walking stick entered the church. She asked if this was the church of St Gerasimos and if she could be directed to his icon, which she addressed in this way:

> Dear Saint, I didn't know you. I'd never heard of you. I hadn't even heard your name. And yet you did me the honour of visiting me and you asked me to bring the walking stick I had bought in Jerusalem to your house. And here I've brought it to you, my dear Saint. You said, 'I want you to bring me the walking stick tomorrow morning!' I didn't know where you were, but I asked and now I've found you.

'Can you believe it?' said St Porphyrios, who received the walking stick from the woman. 'It's truly miraculous. The saint took care of someone as insignificant as myself!'

Natalia Andreyeva was born in Russia in 1834, the daughter of an agricultural serf. When she was about forty-five years old, she developed a serious inflammation of the joints as a result of a severe chill and was practically incapable of walking, even with crutches. In 1887, she had a dream in which the Mother of God appeared to her carrying the child Jesus and urging her to make pilgrimage to the Monastery of Valamo. In the church of the Dormition of the Mother of God, she found an icon that depicted the Theotokos exactly as she had seen her in the dream. On returning home she found her condition much improved. She went to Valamo again, but this time could not find the icon in the place where she had seen it previously or anywhere else in the monastery, because the monks disliked its rather daring modern style and it had been consigned to a storeroom in the early 1890s. In 1897, Natalia made a third visit and prayed on her arrival that she would be able to find the icon that she had so loved but had been unable to find again. As the result of another vision, the icon was found in the church's storeroom and it was brought to the lower church, that Natalia might pray in front of it. She now recovered entirely from the disease that had afflicted her for nearly twenty years. The monks made a written record of the discovery of the icon and of Natalia Andreyeva's miraculous recovery. The icon now achieved great popularity and the icon workshop produced copies and printed reproductions, though the church authorities refused permission for a book as the icon had not been officially recognized as wonder-working. Hieromonk Alipi, who had painted the icon, basing it on two ancient styles, the Mother of God Panagia, 'The All-Holy', and *Nikopoeia*, 'The Victorious', now painted a copy for the monastery's town house in St Petersburg and gave it an inscription in which it was called the 'naturally miracle-working icon of the All-Holy Mother of God of Valamo'. The Valamo monastery was in Finland from 1917. The icon was among the moveable items removed during 1939–1940 as the Soviet Army invaded Finland and it is now in the church of the New Valamo monastery belonging to the Orthodox Church of Finland.

Collections of miracle stories circulated in Russia as part of the campaign to canonize the family of Tsar Nicholas II. In one narrative a woman called Nina Kartashova tells how, when she was ill with pneumonia, she saw a young nurse, aged about seventeen, in her bedroom. The nurse gave her name as Maria and spoke with a Petersburg accent. She covered the sick woman with an officer's greatcoat, which she said belonged to her Papa, and remarked: 'You'll be quite well today. Papa told me. Today it's his birthday.' When Nina Kartashova awoke the next morning, she found a branch of fresh lilac in a vase and a rosary or prayer rope that had belonged to her late grandmother and been buried with her hanging on an icon of Christ in her bedroom.

Miracles of this sort do not come as a direct answer to prayer but from the person's need being known to God 'who knows our needs before we ask'. This reinforces the fundamental faith in the God who loves us and encourages devotion, without creating a causal link between devotion and miracle. The initiative belongs to God.

These five features – beauty, boundaries, asceticism, biography and miracle – are among the elements that, after faith, give Orthodoxy something of its distinctive character. Other observers of the Orthodox Church would doubtless identify different defining features. Introducing her translation of the Kiev Caves *Paterikon*, Muriel Heppell explains that the book mixes fact, legend partly based on fact, borrowings from previous lives of the Fathers (which she calls 'literary plagiarisms') and pure invention. She does not weigh the parts to tell us how much we get of each, but she does argue that all of it, including the many stories of miracles, enables the modern reader to understand the *Weltanschauung*, the 'world view', of the authors and their audience. What sort of world did they see? It was, she says, one in which (a) people expected miracles to happen and (b) they were keenly aware of the influence of non-material forces. She expands this second section so that it includes the:

1 assaults of demons;
2 constant vigilance of angels;
3 compassionate intercession of the Theotokos;
4 peculiar strength of a holy man;
5 and, above all else, the power of God to intervene at any time and in any way in human affairs.

This is a pretty accurate description of the current world-view of Orthodoxy. It is one that makes few concessions to modernity. Late in 2018, a priest posted the text of a sermon on social media. He did not explain why he delivered it, but what he says is a clear affirmation of the boundary between what is and what is not Orthodox, with which most Orthodox Christians would agree:

> I am taking it for granted that an Orthodox Christian will be Orthodox on purpose and will be actively pro-Orthodox, pro-Holy Tradition and on board with the Orthodox Church in general. However, if you take the view that the Church of Christ is open to modification or revision; that we need to modernize, become more relevant to society or change with the times then perhaps you need to rediscover your Orthodoxy and embrace it on purpose.

3

The wedding garment

Repentance is a key theme in Orthodoxy. It is not the act of a single moment but something continuous and part of the fundamental structure of what it means to be a Christian. At its simplest it means recognizing that one has sinned, acknowledging one's responsibility and seeking forgiveness. It is summed up in the Greek word *metanoia*. This signifies a complete change and renewal of heart and mind. It is the exercise of free will in order to recover the divine image in its pristine state. As the Christian recovers the image first in baptism, so repentance enables that image to be preserved. A person cannot baptize him- or herself. Baptism is a sacrament administered by the Church and repentance also has an ecclesial character, found both in the sacrament of confession and in the liturgy. The Church directs the Christian soul, teaching, guiding, exhorting and rebuking according to necessity. A noted representative of Russian lay spirituality, Prince Vladimir Monomakh, who died in 1125, taught in his *Admonition*, addressed to his sons, that salvation requires repentance with tears and charity. His writing indicates a clear predilection for the prayers of Lent, a preference that has always been shared by the Russian people, as George Fedotov observed. It is in Lent and Pre-Lent that we are reminded in the words of St Paul (1 Corinthians 10.12) that those who stand should take heed lest they fall. On the Sunday of the Publican and the Pharisee, right at the beginning of the Pre-Lent season, the text of the divine office dramatically contrasts the proud words of the Pharisee, 'I thank you, God, that I am not like other people,' with the humble, contrite prayer of the Publican, 'Lord, have mercy on me, a sinner', and the Church prays, 'Open unto me, O Giver of Life, the gates of repentance.' Repentance is essential in the Orthodox understanding of Christianity. It brings together, and so illumines, a number of aspects of the Orthodox faith. In it the various strands – Bible, tradition, the Fathers, liturgy, asceticism and spirituality – are intertwined. This chapter, following the path of repentance, explores this interaction, focusing specifically on a significant image derived from the parables of Jesus that is employed in the liturgy and expounded by the Fathers: the wedding garment of Matthew 22.

Beginning with Scripture, we find, among the many examples from the Old Testament, that the one most cited is the repentance of King David when accused by the prophet Nathan after the king's adultery with Bathsheba and the murder of her husband Uriah the Hittite, as narrated in 2 Samuel 12.1–25. To this can be added the repentance of King Ahab after Elijah accused him over the death of Naboth and the seizure of his vineyard, in 1 Kings 21.27–29; of the young King Manasseh in 2 Chronicles 33.9–13 and in the Prayer of Manasseh; of the prophet Daniel's prayer for himself and his people in Daniel 9.1–19; and of the repentance of the people of Nineveh, in sackcloth and ashes, on hearing the preaching of Jonah (Jonah 3.6–10). St John Chrysostom, in his nine homilies on repentance preached in Antioch in the years 386 or 387, contrasts those who 'admit the sin to annul it' with Cain, who was, he says, punished 'not so much for murder as for his impudence'. If he had confessed at once he would have been the first, by this means, to erase his sin. Several times Chrysostom quotes the text of Isaiah 43.26 in a Greek version that reads, 'Be the first one to tell of your transgressions so you may be justified.' St Athanasius teaches, in his letter to Marcellinus, that 'the whole of human existence, both the dispositions of the soul and the movements of the thoughts, have been measured out and encompassed in [the] very words of the Psalter'. We would, therefore, expect to find repentance, confession and forgiveness there and we do in a number of psalms, including Psalm 38 (Orthodox 37) and Psalm 51 (50). Psalm 38 (37) is the plea of one who fears God's rebuke and discipline. The title of Psalm 51 (50), the strongest psalm of repentance, links it to David, Bathsheba and Nathan, and this may be true of Psalm 38 (37) too. The Gospels tell us that John the Baptist came preaching repentance. Jesus too proclaims, 'Repent, for the kingdom of heaven is at hand' (Matthew 3.2, 4.17, NRSV). The Apostle Peter calls those who hear him to repentance and baptism 'for the forgiveness of sins' (Acts 2.38, NRSV) and St John teaches that if we confess our sins God is faithful and just to forgive us our sins (1 John 1–9).

As the main route to salvation, repentance presupposes humility. As the parable of the Publican and the Pharisee shows, pride makes repentance impossible or vain. Christ, says the liturgy, has set before us the abasement of the Publican as a path to exaltation and a pattern of how we may be saved. In a litany before the Lord's Prayer, chanted in the Liturgy of St John Chrysostom, the deacon asks that we believers 'may live out the rest of our days in peace and repentance'. We gain a sense of why this is necessary from a text in the Orthodox order for Preparation for Holy Communion:

> How can I who am unworthy dare to come to the Communion of Thy Holy Things? For if I should dare to approach Thee with those that are worthy, my garment betrayeth me, for it is not a festal robe, and I shall cause the condemnation of my greatly-sinful soul.

The language of filthiness, impurity and pollution, of the defaced image and the defilement of flesh and spirit used in the prayers preparatory to receiving communion, may seem in the modern age to be so much hyperbole as the awesome holiness of the Sacrament is compared to the utter unworthiness of the would-be recipient by Basil the Great, John Chrysostom, Symeon Metaphrastes, John Damascene and Symeon the New Theologian. The full weight of patristic teaching, however, affirms the unworthiness and insufficiency of those who stand before the very doors of the temple, yet do not put away evil thoughts. The same teaching offers reassurance that Christ receives the penitent. He justified the Publican, had mercy on the Canaanite woman, opened the doors of paradise to the thief, received the sinful woman who washed His feet and healed the woman with the issue of blood.

Underlying the prayers and devotions of the Orthodox liturgy is the whole theology of creation, fall, redemption and fulfilment. The twentieth-century dogmatic theologian Vladimir Lossky observed that in theology all themes converge and co-penetrate and each theme receives meaning from being surrounded by the entire truth. The eucharistic encounter is seen as a foretaste of the eschatological banquet, the marriage feast. If, then, we are unworthy to receive communion now, how can we ever be worthy to enter heaven? This sense of being present at the feast but being unworthy is set out most clearly in the final section of the parable in Matthew 22, usually called the parable of the wedding feast, in which Jesus said that the Kingdom of heaven might be compared to a king who gave a wedding banquet for his son. When those who were invited refused to come and mistreated the messengers, the king issued a general invitation and his slaves went out into the streets and gathered all whom they found, both good and bad, so that the wedding hall was filled with guests. This makes an excellent parable of the Kingdom. Those chosen, the people of the old covenant, are not worthy, and in their stead the festal hall of the heavenly banquet is filled with any who would come. All are welcome and the hall is full, and this sounds like the Kingdom of heaven as we might want or imagine it to be, but the parable does not end here. At the conclusion Jesus said that the king came in to see his guests. As he looked around, he noticed a man who was there at the wedding feast but was not wearing a wedding robe. The king said to him, 'Friend, how did you get in here without a wedding robe?' The man was speechless. The king summoned the attendants and ordered them to bind him hand and foot and to throw him into the outer darkness, where, we are told, there will be weeping and gnashing of teeth, and Jesus adds, 'For many are called, but few are chosen.'

In order to understand this text from Matthew we will look first at the interpretation of the parable of the wedding feast and then at the use made of it in the Liturgy. Cyril of Jerusalem (313–386) uses a version of the parable in his *Catechetical Lectures*. He detaches the section about the wedding garment from the rest of the parable and supplies his own account of how the guest pushed his way into a wedding party and took his place at the banquet, but though he saw how the other guests were dressed he did not himself change his garments. It is the bridegroom who asks him about it and, having explained that he should have taken the opportunity to withdraw and to come back suitably dressed, says that as he came in unceremoniously so he would be thrown out unceremoniously. He then orders the servants, 'Bind his feet, which had the hardihood to bring him here. Bind his hands that could not dress him properly. And throw him out into darkness, for he does not deserve wedding lights.' It is in the Pro-catechesis that Cyril says this – that is, before he properly begins the preparation for baptism. He tells those who have by their own decision been enrolled as catechumens that if they have come with a purpose that is anything but pure, they should withdraw now and return the next day wearing a different dress: not the robe of uncleanness, but the brilliant robe of self-discipline. He stresses too that this new robe cannot be put on over the old one; the old one must be stripped off.

Gregory of Nyssa (d. *c.* 395), writing on virginity, says that if a man is to take Wisdom as a helpmate and life-companion, then 'he will prepare himself in a manner worthy of such a love, so as to feast with all the joyous wedding guests in spotless raiment, and not be cast forth, while claiming to sit at that feast, for not having put on the wedding garment' and then adds, tellingly, that it is plain this argument applies equally to men and women, quoting the Apostle Paul when he writes, 'There is neither male nor female. Christ is all, and in all.' John Chrysostom himself (d. 407), when preaching on Matthew 22, merely refers to the garment as 'life and practice', but in another homily, he compares two garments – that woven with gold and worn by the queen and the filthy garment at the wedding feast – and says, 'Therefore the prophet saith concerning her "The queen did stand upon thy right hand in a vesture woven with gold." He does not mean a real vesture, but virtue. Therefore the Scripture elsewhere saith "How camest thou in hither not having a wedding garment?" so that here he does not mean a garment, but fornication, and foul and unclean living.'

Augustine of Hippo (354–430), whose spiritual insights may be preferred to his theology, preached at length on the parable. This is from the relevant section of the homily. The servants invite all to the feast without further scrutiny. It is the master of the house who finds the one without a wedding garment. The garment that is looked for is in the heart and not on the body. What is the wedding garment? It is not baptism, for both the good and the bad have been baptized. It is not the Holy Communion, for many eat and in doing so, 'eat and drink judgment to themselves'. It is not fasting and it is not miracles. Having told his congregation what it is not, he says, quoting 1 Timothy, that it is charity which comes out of a pure heart, a good conscience and faith unfeigned. The wedding garment is charity, and we see here the connection to the Eucharist. It is a sermon preached at the Liturgy, and Augustine says he is addressing those who are already within, that is to say in the banqueting hall, who are approaching the feast and still do not have the garment that honours the Bridegroom and honours the union between Christ the Bridegroom and the Church, Christ's Bride.

As in other of his homilies, Gregory the Dialogist, Pope of Rome from 590 to his death in 604, largely followed Augustine, beginning with a warning to his hearers that they have already come into the house of the marriage feast, our holy Church, as a result of God's generosity and must be careful, 'lest when the King enters he find fault with some aspect of [their] heart's clothing'. The wedding garment is love, and Gregory is surprised and saddened that anyone should appear in contemptible clothing among those rejoicing and celebrating the festive occasion. Like a garment woven with two pieces of wool, an upper and a lower, so the wedding garment must combine love of God and love of neighbour. The one who lacks the garment is called 'friend' by the king: not *a friend*, as if he were saying, 'friend because of your faith, not a friend because of your actions'. In the face of this strict and final chastisement, nothing can be said and the guest is silent. Bound already by sin, he is now bound in punishment; with blindness of heart making for inner darkness, he is cast into the eternal night of condemnation, outer darkness.

Pope Leo the Great (*c.* 400–461; Pope from 440) refers to the parable in a letter to the clergy and people of Constantinople and takes rather a different approach. The one who does not believe that the only-begotten Son of God assumed our human nature in Mary's womb is 'without share in the Mystery of the Christian religion, and as he neither recognizes the Bridegroom nor knows the Bride, can have no place at the wedding banquet'. He calls the flesh of Christ 'the veil of the Word' and it is in this veil that everyone is clothed who confesses Christ unreservedly. The one who is ashamed of the flesh and rejects it as unworthy of Christ will not be so adorned and, if present unseasonably at the sacred banquet, will be found out and cast out. This is one of the strongest patristic assertions concerning the body, in which Leo says, 'whosoever confesses not the human body in Christ must know that he is unworthy of the mystery of the Incarnation'.

We find a similar understanding among the desert ascetics. In the alphabetical collection of the sayings of the Desert Fathers we read of Abba Dioscurus, one of four Egyptian monks in Nitria known as the Four Tall Brothers, who were involved in a dispute over the theologian Origen and the troubles of John Chrysostom. He is recorded as saying:

> If we wear our heavenly robe, we shall not be found naked, but if we are found not wearing this garment, what shall we do, brothers? We, even we also, shall hear the voice that says, 'Cast them into outer darkness; there men will weep and gnash their teeth.' [Matthew 22.13] And, brothers, there will be great shame in store for us, if, after having worn this [monk's] habit for so long, we are found in the hour of need not having put on the wedding garment. Oh what compunction will seize us! What darkness will fall upon us, in the presence of our fathers and our brothers, who will see us being tortured by the angels of punishment!

Included in the classic anthology of ascetical spirituality, the *Philokalia,* Evagrios the Solitary (also known as Evagrios Ponticus,

345–399) describes the offending garment in Matthew 22 as being woven of impure thoughts and says that the true wedding garment is 'the dispassion of the deiform soul which has renounced worldly desires'. In the ninth century this line is repeated by Theodoros the Great Ascetic, who adds that it is through intercourse with shameful passions that the soul discards its robe of self-restraint and debases itself by wearing rags and tatters, which may well be a paraphrase of a similar observation by Maximus the Confessor (590–662). The so-called Makarian Homilies, from the fourth century, simply describe the wedding garment as the grace of the Holy Spirit; the one not worthy of wearing it has no part in the celestial marriage and in the spiritual wedding feast.

These examples give something of the flavour of a patristic interpretation and demonstrate a certain fluidity in the interpretation of a difficult passage. The wedding garment becomes a powerful metaphor for what makes us acceptable to God, and the stained garment for everything that gives rise to negative judgement and punishment. There is not a single view, but we can see quite clearly the connection to the Eucharist as the type of the heavenly banquet, the need for right action as well as right belief, and the way in which love or charity provides a fitting garment for the soul, whereas seeking one's own interests rather than Christ's, or being given over to vice rather than virtue, makes the inner garment filthy and unacceptable. The moral understanding becomes the dominant one. Leo alone, it seems, places the stress on right belief and makes of the wedding garment something that is not acquired by moral action but by mystical union with Christ. In a sermon preached at the beginning of Lent in 859 or 860, Patriarch Photius of Constantinople combines St Paul's teaching about 'putting on Christ', like a garment, and being members of Christ with the bridal imagery, when he says:

Indeed, as many of us as have been baptized into Christ have put on Christ (Gal. 3.27) and have become members of Christ; for we have learnt from the divine Paul's teaching that our bodies are members of Christ (1 Cor. 6.15). What then of us?

Have we preserved our bridal condition unsoiled, not letting it be polluted by any evil?

John of Kronstadt teaches the importance of approaching the Eucharist with prepared, pure, elevated souls, 'in order not to be amongst the number of those who have no wedding garment, but a garment defiled by the passions'. John Climacus issues a warning that is significant in its requirement for constant and life-long spiritual vigilance. 'Never be overly confident,' he writes, 'until you hear the final judgment against yourself, keeping in mind the wedding guest who made it as far as attending the wedding, but then was tied up, hand and foot, and cast into outer darkness.'

Mother Marina demonstrates how this text affects Orthodox monastic spirituality when writing about a year in the life of the Finnish Convent of the Holy Trinity, Lintula. She says this:

A nun pursues the ascetic life in order to gain salvation, and in this she needs the company of others who are engaged in the same way of life in order that they can strive towards this goal together. Jesus Christ suffered for us, but we cannot bear even the slightest offence without rancour. Do we not feel pain in our heart when we sing during Holy Week, 'I see thy bridal chamber adorned, O my Saviour, and I have no wedding garment that I may enter there'? How have our own preparations for the feast of the Resurrection of our Lord progressed?

All of this comes from formal teaching, from catechesis, homilies, biblical commentary and ascetical instruction. By contrast, the Church's liturgy is not communicating formal teaching to its participants. It is addressing God, and the words used are addressed by the participants to God. The liturgy is a source of primary theology, but this is not its basic purpose. We can certainly find in the liturgical texts multiple references to the stained garment: the raiment of shame, the defiled garment, the filthy garments of my sins, the loathsome garment of self-indulgence, the deceitful robe of hypocrisy, the garments of death. We find these contrasted with the glorious robe of divine Beauty, the shining robe of abstinence, the robe of holiness and the shining raiment of regeneration. It is perhaps surprising, given the nature of the baptismal rite, that there are few references to the baptismal robe. There is one explicit confession that 'I have stained the robe with which I was clothed in Holy Baptism', together with rather clever use of the imagery from the parable of Dives and Lazarus (Luke 16.19–31) that, addressing Christ, refers to 'the fine linen of baptism and the purple of thy blood', thus picking up on an idea that Christ, naked on the cross, was actually clothed in his own blood. There are a further set of texts in the liturgy that represent a different strand. Some of these refer to a first garment woven by the Creator, others speak not of one garment replacing another or of a garment being stained and defiled, but of being stripped naked by sin. The other notable omission is any use of the multiple texts concerning garments to be found in the book of the Revelation, which is explained by the very late point of that book's admission to the canon in the East, such that it is never read or actually quoted in the liturgy.

There are two major liturgical texts that refer to the stained garment. The first of these is the eighth-century Great Canon of St Andrew of Crete (d. 740), sung at Great Compline on the first four days of Lent and in its entirety at the end of the Great Fast, which is a dialogue between Andrew and his soul. It is Andrew who declares:

I have stained the garment of my flesh, O Saviour, and defiled that which was made in Thine image and likeness.

And again:

I have torn the first garment that the Creator wove for me in the beginning and now lie naked.
I have clothed myself in the torn coat that the serpent wove for me by his counsel, and I am ashamed.

The Canon refers to the robe woven by God being stripped away by sin and being replaced by garments of skin. It also speaks of the raiment of shame and a garment 'defiled and shamefully blood-stained by a life of passion and self-indulgence', a many-coloured coat of shameful thoughts. Together with this goes the loss of the beauty and glory with which human beings were first created. Andrew's Canon also refers to the bridal chamber and the parable in Matthew 22, when he says:

> I am deprived of the bridal chamber, of the wedding and the supper; for want of oil my lamp has gone out; while I slept the door was closed; the supper had been eaten; I am bound hand and foot, and cast out.

This combined theme of the bridal chamber and the wedding garment repeats in the days before Palm Sunday and it is a major theme at the start of Great and Holy Week, with Monday to Wednesday being known as days of the Bridegroom. This text, sung three times, slowly and solemnly on each day, expands the theme of the bridal chamber:

> I see Thy bridal chamber adorned, O my Saviour, and I have no wedding garment that I may enter there. Make the robe of my soul to shine, O Giver of Light, and save me.

The services at the start of Great Week take up, repeat and develop a number of related motifs. One of these is the chastity of Jacob's son Joseph in Egypt. The text makes the Egyptian woman, known to us as Potiphar's wife, into a second Eve, one flattered by the serpent into seeking to make Joseph fall. Joseph, however, fled from sin, leaving his garment behind him, and 'like the first man before his disobedience, though naked, he was not ashamed'. The texts point out that, after his disobedience, knowing he was naked, Adam clothed himself in shame with fig leaves, and then reminds us that at the judgement we will all stand naked before the Judge (that is to say, unable to hide anything). There are three related Bridegroom themes in these days: first, the coming of the Bridegroom in the middle of the night and the need to be watchful; second, the virgins with their lamps, divided into those who 'overflow with the oil of compassion' who enter the bridal chamber and those who have no oil and find the door closed; and third, a conflation of the wedding banquet and the bridal chamber, with the soiled wedding garment. As these are combined we get a sense of the Bridegroom coming, which is, or should be, a source of joy; like the virgins, we go out to meet him and we see the furnished bridal chamber, but then realize that we, through our own fault, lack the wedding garment that must be worn if we are to enter.

The second text of significance is one used on the Friday before Palm Sunday, which is attributed to the Emperor Leo VI, the Wise, who died in 912. It gives a quite specific meaning to the wedding garment and is the fullest and most coherent exposition of the text:

> Despising the divine commands, my soul, thou hast become an easy prey to the snares of the enemy; and by thine own choice thou hast surrendered thyself to corruption. Sunk in slumber through thy many trespasses, thou hast covered with filth the garment that God wove for thee, and made thyself unfit for the wedding of the King; and thou shalt be dragged away because of thy sin. For if thou sittest at the wedding feast clad in the raiment of the passions, He will ask thee how thou camest in, and thou shalt be cast out from the bridal chamber. But cry to the Saviour: O dread eye of God, Thou hast become what I am, without ceasing to be who Thou wast. Before Thy Crucifixion, for my sake Thou hast worn a robe of mockery: tear in pieces my sackcloth and clothe me with gladness; deliver me from the outer darkness and eternal weeping, and have mercy upon me.

Here we see the Orthodox understanding of human sinfulness and redemption. There is no Orthodox doctrine of inherited original sin. For the Orthodox, human beings have exercised their own free choice in refusing to follow the will of God. Such a refusal is habitual, characterized as laxness, as being sunk in slumber, such that one is unaware of one's own corruption. We see also that human life must have an eschatological orientation, meaning that it must be directed towards the fulfilment of God's promises when Christ comes in glory and in judgement (the coming of the Bridegroom) with a very strong sense that the judgement may go against the soul and that the remedy for this is repentance. We see also that the soul begins with a garment of some sort woven by God, but that this garment, now covered in filth, is not suitable for a wedding. Christ, who before His crucifixion wore the robe of mockery, can tear the inadequate garment of sackcloth into pieces, clothe the soul with gladness and deliver it from outer darkness and eternal weeping.

There is nothing systematic or dogmatic about this. The Greek lay theologian Panayiotis Nellas points to the way in which the Fathers used the phrase 'in the image of God' to express the reality of the natural human condition without constructing a system around this truth; they also used the concept of garments to describe and interpret the state of humankind after the biblical fall, but again in an unsystematic way. The Orthodox tradition resists the imposition of a single scheme of ideas. Vladimir Lossky warns that a theology that constitutes itself as a system 'is always dangerous: it imprisons in a closed sphere of thought that toward which, on the contrary, thought should open itself'. And this openness, this lack of system, may show itself to be the true strength of Orthodox theology.

Despite many and timely warnings about presumption, Orthodox theology is imbued with hope as can be shown with a final liturgical quotation. It is from the vesting prayers of the eucharistic Liturgy of St John Chrysostom and demonstrates that in Orthodoxy salvation is a present reality and the Eucharist a foretaste of heaven:

My soul shall rejoice in the Lord, for He hath put upon me the robe of salvation, and has clothed me with the garment of gladness. He hath set a crown upon my head, like unto a bridegroom; and as a bride has adorned me with comeliness.

4

Heaven on earth

'The Eastern Liturgy,' wrote the Russian historian G. P. Fedotov, 'is one of the most beautiful and original creations of Byzantine culture.' The life of Georgii Petrovich Fedotov divides into three parts: the Russian, the French and the American. Born in Russia in 1886, he lived and studied in St Petersburg until 1925; he was in Paris as an émigré from 1925 until 1940, and taught Latin, church history and hagiology at the St Sergius Orthodox Theological Institute; he emigrated to the United States in 1940, where he adopted a modified name and a new persona. He was now Professor George P. Fedotov of St Vladimir's Seminary, formerly a fellow at Yale, an American citizen and best known as the author of *The Russian Religious Mind: Kievan Christianity*, published by Harvard University Press in 1946. In it he describes the Byzantine liturgy in this way:

> The beauty of the Byzantine cult is expressed in words and gestures, in liturgical vestments, in dramatic actions, in choral song and icon paintings, as well as in sacred architecture. The particular style of Byzantine beauty can be defined as baroque, used in its largest sense. It is solemn, magnificent, overladen with ornaments, resplendent with gold and precious stones. It is properly a palace style with, however, mystical depth beneath it. In fact, the Byzantine temple is, at the same time, the palace of God and the *adytum* [inner shrine] of mysteries.

In Fedotov's view, the early church was the heir of both the Synagogue and the Hellenistic mystery rites. From the former came the psalm type of prayer and Scripture reading; from the latter came the framework of the mysteries in words and symbolic actions. The mysteries belong to the few, to the initiates, but the Gospel belonged to all including the unlettered masses. There was danger in such vulgarization and the Church responded by protecting and hiding the Christian mysteries. A prayer before communion expresses this hidden aspect when it says:

> Accept me this day, O Son of God, for a sharer of thy mystic Supper; for I will not tell the secret to thine enemies; I will not give thee a kiss, like Judas; but like the robber I confess Thee: Remember me, O Lord, in thy Kingdom.

There is a secret at the heart of the Liturgy, a mystery only partially unfolded, the full meaning of which is only available to the faithful Orthodox. The Church placed boundaries around the secret by saying some prayers inaudibly and by hiding the sanctuary behind the icon screen, doors and curtain. The imperial palace also influenced the shape of worship with the adoption and adaption of court ceremonies and formulas and silk and gold vestments. Fedotov believes that even after more than a thousand years and on foreign Slavic soil, the Constantinopolitan palace still lives in every Orthodox Church and particularly in the cathedral. The vesting of a bishop at the beginning of a hierarchical Liturgy closely follows the ceremony of the emperor's dressing. Fedotov suggests that the Orthodox service gives an impression of God's presence in His temple, in His mysteries, icons and relics: God's presence in sacred matter. That impression is often referred to as one of heaven on earth, or more precisely of heaven descending to earth. He thinks that the most essential emotion of the Orthodox faithful at worship is not longing or joy, but fear and exaltation.

> Man, sinful and unworthy man, is called to contemplate the Divine glory. He stands in the palace of the Heavenly King who is imagined seated upon the throne behind the Iconostasis, seeing everything in man's heart and mind. The contrition, self-humiliation, fear, and beseeching of man on the one side,

and the radiant glory of God on the other: between these two religious poles runs the whole gamut of liturgical emotions.

Fedotov asks how far the Byzantine liturgy in Slavonic translation was accessible to the newly converted Russian. His answer is significant for all who understand little of Orthodox liturgical language. He thinks that the worshipper's general impression of the service was more of actions, tunes and pictures than of the words and ideas that shaped the Russian soul. He sums it up in a memorable line, 'The impression was overwhelming but vague.' The worshipper, now as then, becomes accustomed to ever-recurring words and phrases; fragments of ideas are dimly perceived and a seed is sown. Regularly attending services in Church Slavonic, one first becomes aware of such recurring responses as 'Gospodi pomilui' ('Lord, have mercy') and 'Slava Tebe Bozhe' ('Glory to Thee, O God'). The next most noticed is probably a text that is strongly reinforced by its chant, the Trisagion: 'Svyatyi Bozhe, Svyatyi Krepkii, Svyatyi Bezsmertnyi, pomilui nas' ('Holy God, Holy and Mighty, Holy and Immortal, have mercy upon us'). These frequently recurrent phrases reinforce Fedotov's sense that glory and fear (in the sense of the fear of the Lord) are combined, as when Isaiah said, 'Woe is me, for I have seen the Lord.'

One of the most frequent comments made by the non-Orthodox about the Orthodox liturgy is that it is beautiful but incomprehensible, and so long! In his book about Mount Athos, *Paradise Within Reach*, René Gothóni, a Finnish scholar of the study of religions specializing in monasteries, pilgrimage and hermeneutics, recounts the experience of a German history teacher, a Lutheran, who felt that the monastic services were too long. He said, 'I was tired during the morning service and vespers. One is very tired at three o'clock in the morning and the service seems to last for ever. Again and again they chant monotonously: *Kyrie eleison, Kyrie eleison*. For us this is strange.' Timothy (Kallistos) Ware pointed out, in 1963, that the Orthodox approach religion in a liturgical way. The Church is first of all a worshipping community (he is quoting George Florovsky) and human beings are liturgical creatures 'who are most truly themselves when they glorify God, and who find their perfection and self-fulfilment in worship'. Neither liturgy nor worship were included earlier in the defining characteristics of the Orthodox ethos because other Christian bodies or parts of them (such as the Benedictine Order and Anglican cathedrals, with their strong choral tradition) can also be defined in this way. It surprises regular visitors to Orthodox churches that these long services, sometimes sung in archaic languages with the congregation playing little or no part in the singing and with a screen separating the people from the action at the altar, are popular, communal and even homely. Orthodox writers often compare their own services with what they have themselves experienced of non-Orthodox worship, and more often still with the worst of what they have experienced. This can give rise to lists of *what they do* and of *what we do better*. Not all Orthodox liturgy makes one wonder if it is heaven rather than earth, but it is important to say that poor worship is the exception in Orthodoxy.

Orthodox worship differs in many ways from the services of the most liturgical of non-Orthodox churches. The forms of worship are familiar to Orthodox Christians and they are at ease with them. Some will have a book, generally not in order to follow the service but for prayers before and after communion and other devotions. Books will be more in evidence during Great Week when the services are longer and less familiar. Greek churches in Britain and elsewhere have a Sunday sheet with the readings in Greek and English and two different homilies, one in each language. In her excellent book, *Welcome to the Orthodox Church: An introduction to Eastern Christianity*, the American writer Frederica Mathewes-Green, wife of an Orthodox priest and playing the traditional role of *matushka*, provides a helpful and detailed tour of the imagined church and parish of St Felicity and its life. The picture is of a church that has adapted in some significant practical ways to American ways of doing religion, including the use of English for the liturgy. There are some Anglophone churches and communities in Britain, especially among the Antiochenes, but many parishes have an historic ethnicity and at least part of the liturgy is in old Greek,

Church Slavonic, Serbian, Romanian and so on. An English text of the service will not be much help there. Actually a text is generally a distraction during worship. Do you follow the text or look at what is happening and listen? It is rather like the question posed by surtitles at an opera being sung in its language of composition. Do you follow the titles and miss some of what is going on or focus on the singers and lose some of the meaning? Whatever you choose, it is made easier if you have read a summary of the plot and perhaps become familiar with the music. The surtitles will help you out if you get completely lost. Orthodox liturgy can be a linguistic challenge, if not a sea of linguistic confusion.

The term used for the original of a particular form of icon is 'prototype' and there is a prototype too for the church building. Many Orthodox communities outside of Orthodox countries will serve the Liturgy in buildings that belonged to non-Orthodox Christian bodies and have been adapted. Some of these are in the form of a Latin cross, with square end, transepts and a long nave furnished with pews. It is not an ideal shape for Orthodox Liturgy. Creating an Orthodox sanctuary separated from the nave by a screen with icons is the minimum necessary change if it is to begin to feel authentic. Many Orthodox borrow or share a building belonging to another Christian body and cannot make even that sort of change. They must then resort to the same methods as army chaplains in the Great War, taking a demountable iconostasis with them, putting it up before and taking it down after every service. There is a temporary feel, reinforcing the idea that 'here we have no abiding kingdom', yet Orthodox clergy and laity perceive some sort of historic prototype of what a church building should be like, whether it is some great and highly decorated Byzantine church or one of the main styles of Russian architecture in either wood or stone.

The Orthodox temple

Ideally, an Orthodox church is freestanding to enable it to be circled in procession. Monastic churches in Orthodox countries are not linked to other buildings, such as the cloister, chapter house and dormitory, as they are in the West, but stand alone in the centre of a great courtyard. The entrance, whenever possible, should be at the west end and the sanctuary at the east. Historically churches take many shapes, some of which have been given religious significance. A common shape is an oblong or rectangle that is not as long as most Western churches, but still representative, as the word 'nave' suggests, of a boat to convey believers across stormy seas to a safe harbour. Churches are also often cruciform, to proclaim faith in Christ crucified, though the shape may be more evident inside than out. An Orthodox church may have a dome or cupolas, or a combination of these. There will always be an odd number of these and each has been given significance: one cupola signifies Christ as the head of the Church; three symbolize the Most Holy Trinity; five represent Christ and four Evangelists; seven is said to symbolize the Seven Ecumenical Councils, nine the orders of Angels, and thirteen Christ and the twelve Holy Apostles. Every dome or cupola and the roof itself, if there is no dome, carries a cross, the sign and instrument of salvation. The cross takes many different shapes, but Russian Orthodox churches generally use the so-called three-bar cross, consisting of the usual long crossbeam with a short crossbeam above it and another, near the bottom of the cross, which is at a slant. The top short beam represents the superscription placed above Christ on the cross, written in Hebrew, Greek and Latin, stating, 'Jesus of Nazareth, the King of the Jews'. When this crossbar has letters on it, they are the first letters of each of those words, in Greek 'INBI' and in Latin 'INRI'. The hands of Jesus were nailed to the middle crossbar and His feet to the lower one. A common explanation of the slant of the lower crossbar is that it is pointing heavenward for the so-called Good Thief, crucified on Jesus' right, and towards hell for the thief on His left who mocked Him.

The ideal form of Orthodox church is a cruciform building, with narthex, nave or naos, transepts and sanctuary, and three apses at the east end. Commenting on the Liturgy, the Fathers envisioned the church building as consisting of three parts that were representative of mystical realities. It was Germanus of Constantinople who wrote that the church is an earthly heaven in which the supercelestial God dwells and walks about, and it is more glorious than the [Old Testament] tabernacle of witness. It is foreshadowed in the Patriarchs, is based on the Apostles ... it is foretold by the Prophets, adorned by the Hierarchs, sanctified by the Martyrs, and its high Altar stands firmly founded on their holy remains.

St Symeon the New Theologian explained that 'the [Narthex] corresponds to earth, the [Nave] to heaven, and the holy [Altar] to what is above heaven'. St Symeon of Thessalonica wrote in a similar way that 'the shape of the divine temple also represents what is on earth, what is in heaven, and what is above the heavens'. The symbolism of the church in representing the human being is analysed by St Maximus the Confessor in his *Mystagogia*; the altar represents the spirit, the sanctuary the soul and the nave the body. Conversely, the human body, itself the temple of the Holy Spirit, means the spirit is, as it were, an altar, the soul, a sanctuary, and the body a nave.

The divisions of space are also seen to perpetuate the primitive arrangements by which the three portions of the church were set apart for three separate orders of Christians: the narthex for catechumens (those not yet baptized but being prepared for baptism) and penitents (when public penance was practised); the nave for the faithful; the sanctuary for the clergy and their ministers. Kuvochinsky, translator of the Slavonic liturgy into English, states that *every* Russian church consists of *four* portions.

1 The Sanctuary or Altar beyond the Image Screen (iconostasis)
2 The Choir, which consists of two parts
   (a) the Tribune immediately in front of the Holy Door in the centre of the screen;
   (b) the railed places for the choirs on either side of the Tribune.
3 The Nave
4 The Western Porch.

The choirs tend to have moved away into galleries in a number of churches, but otherwise Kuvochinsky's description of the way in which the space in a church is divided is the more accurate of the two. The space between the people in the nave and the iconostasis, which he calls 'the Tribune', is also known as the *solea* and is a significant space for liturgical activity. In ancient times the doorkeepers stood in the porch to prevent certain types of penitents and non-Christians from entering the church proper. Inside the church there was first a spacious vestibule, known as the narthex (in Greek *lity*, in Russian *pritvor*). This is where the catechumens preparing for Initiation received instruction and where penitents who were excluded from Communion stood as well. The baptismal font stood by the door, and certain services (Compline, Midnight Service and the Hours) took place there. The narthex is still used for these services in monasteries and is to be found in modern church buildings as a place for cloakrooms and the candle stall. Historically, there were doors between the narthex and the nave as the icon screen (iconostasis) separates the sanctuary from the nave.

Technically, the word 'nave' is better applied to the longitudinally planned space of the early Christian basilica, and the word 'naos', from the ancient Greek word for temple, implies a more centrally planned space. The usual Orthodox term for a church building is actually 'temple'. There are often seats, even pews, in Orthodox churches in the West, but in traditional churches there are no seats except for a few placed by pillars and some benches placed along the walls. The floor may have rugs or a series of long carpet runners. Open space is easier than fixed and constrictive seating for the bows and prostrations that are a frequent part of worship. The walls of the nave may be decorated with frescoes of the major events in the life of Christ and His Most Pure Mother and of the saints or else there will be icons along the walls, and many will have hanging oil-filled lamps (lampada). Towards the iconostasis there are usually tall banners with iconic images that will be carried in procession like ancient military banners. There will also be icons on sloping stands, known as analoy, and their associated candle stands. In Slavic churches there will be a central analoy with the icon of the Resurrection, of the dedication of the church or feast of the day.

At the east end, behind the iconostasis, is the sanctuary, also sometimes called 'the Altar', and historically called 'the bema', and it contains the Holy Table. Depending on the size and design of the building there may be two small rooms serving as the Prothesis (for the preparation of the bread and wine for the Liturgy) and a vestry. There may be a separate door from the nave to the vestry and another from the vestry to the sanctuary. There is often a way out from the vestry too. The sanctuary usually forms a platform two or more steps higher than the nave. The iconostasis is set back from the edge of the platform to provide a raised space, known as the solea (an elevated place) where communion is administered and where the deacon and other clergy stand for prayers and to address the people. On either side of the solea are places for two choirs, one on each side, though choirs, as already noted, are often on just one side or in a gallery. Greek churches often have a pulpit (ambo) from which the Gospel is read and sermons are given. When the bishop serves the Liturgy a raised platform, called the cathedra, may be placed in the centre of the nave, with an eagle rug on it, where the bishop stands when he is vested and for various parts of the service. In Greek churches there is generally a throne for the bishop on the south side towards the choir.

Architectural historian Robert Ousterhout explains that the Byzantine church changed to conform to what he calls 'the necessities of the mature Byzantine worship service'.

There were really two performance areas. The more sacred activities were restricted to the bema, centred on the altar, while other activities took place in the central space of the naos. The solea and ambo had been eliminated, and the processional nature of the Early Christian service had been eliminated, which helps explain the transformation from the longitudinally planned basilica to the centrally planned naos. The liturgy was reduced to a series of appearances, and for most of the service the templon effectively separated the clergy and the congregation. The centrally positioned naos dome highlighted the ceremonial appearance of the celebrants.

Active participation of the congregation was greatly decreased. The service began with antiphons rather than processions, and it ended with the distribution of sanctified bread rather than communion, which was celebrated only rarely.

Ousterhout does not mean that the Liturgy was rarely celebrated, but the people rarely received communion. His explanation of the architectural changes goes a long way towards explaining why the instructions for the Liturgy refer to spaces or furniture that no longer exist. The most obvious example of this is the prayer near to the end of the Liturgy still called 'the prayer behind the ambo', though there is no ambo for the priest to be behind.

The iconostasis

The most prominent feature of an Orthodox church today is the screen with its icons. It has a central double door, called the Holy Doors or sometimes the Royal Doors, though originally these were the doors from the narthex to the nave. It also has doors towards the end on each side, known as the Deacon's Doors. The Holy Doors may also have a curtain that can be drawn across. The original form of the screen, known as a templon, was not solid in the manner of the iconostasis, but more open. An example of this is the screen in the Church of San Marco in Venice, which has many of the characteristics of a church in Constantinople. In time, the templon became more opaque and held the major icons of the church.

The iconostasis also has a symbolic meaning. It is seen as the boundary between two worlds: the divine and the human, paradise and earth, the permanent and the transitory. The holy icons denote that the Saviour, His Mother and the saints, whom they represent, abide both in heaven and on earth. In this way the iconostasis both divides the divine world from the human world and also unites these same two worlds into one whole, a single place where all separation is overcome and where reconciliation between God and humankind is achieved. Standing on the boundary between the divine and the human, the iconostasis reveals, by means of its icons, the ways to this reconciliation.

The smaller Orthodox churches rarely have an elaborate iconostasis, but there are certain minimum requirements: an icon of Christ the Saviour to the right of the Holy Doors and the Theotokos with the Christ-child to the left. On the doors there will be an icon of the Annunciation, the archangel on the left door, the Blessed Virgin on the right, together with the four Evangelists, two on each door. Over the doors is generally placed an icon of the Last Supper. If there is room the icon of the dedication of the church (patron saint or event) is placed to the right of Christ and another icon of local significance may be placed to the left of the Theotokos. On the Deacon's Doors there are icons of holy deacons, such as St Stephen the Protomartyr, or of angels who minister at the heavenly altar. The screen is surmounted centrally by a cross, which is over the doors. There are clear iconographic schemes for the placing of more icons and indeed for the decoration of the whole church, including the central dome. Some churches are fully decorated with frescoes that follow an iconographic scheme.

The Altar and its furnishings

The Altar (or sanctuary) which lies beyond the iconostasis is set aside for those who perform the services. Other people only enter by invitation, and normally only men are permitted to enter, though on occasion nuns may be seen to pass through the Deacon's Doors. On the central chord of the apse is the Holy Table, which is a freestanding cube of about 80–110 centimetres (31–43 inches). It is completely covered by two cloths: one of white linen, representing the winding-sheet in which Christ's Body was wrapped, and the other, the outer cloth, of bright, rich material representing the glory of God's throne. The Holy Table is said to represent both the throne of God and the tomb of Christ.

At the rear of the Table is placed the Ark (or Tabernacle), which often takes the shape of a small church, within which are placed the Holy Gifts used throughout the year for the communion of the sick.

Behind the Holy Table there is usually a seven-branched candle stand with seven oil lights, and behind that there is often a large processional cross. There will generally be two candlesticks on the Table, a hand-held cross, used for various blessings, and the large Book of the Gospels. This book, which is carried in at the Little Entrance and used for reading the Gospel during the Liturgy, is usually richly adorned with a cover of precious metal and jewels representing Christ and the Evangelists. It is never bound in leather (that is, the skins of dead animals). Also on the Table is a vessel containing the Holy Chrism used for Chrismation, and also a box with all that is needed for taking communion to the sick (a small chest for the Holy Gifts, a small chalice and spoon, a small vessel for wine and a sponge with which to clean the chalice). During Great Lent, a small chest, called the artophorion, is placed on the Holy Table; it contains the consecrated Lambs used for the Presanctified Liturgy, if the tabernacle is not used for this. A book stand is sometimes placed on the Table for the priest to use, or a lectern for the liturgical books may stand adjacent to the north-west corner of the Table.

Behind the Holy Table is a raised place, called the High Place (or bema), on which is placed the bishop's throne, with seats for the priests on either side. When the bishop is present the priests (representing the Holy Apostles) sit at either side of the bishop (representing the King of Glory), but when he is not present the throne is left empty. On either side of the bishop's throne are placed the ceremonial Fans, metal discs carrying representations of the six-winged Seraphim. Once used to fan away insects, they are now carried in solemn processions and may be held over the Gospel book or festive icon by servers during the Liturgy. Above the High Place on the wall behind the Holy Table is an icon of Christ, before which a lamp burns, and on each side icons of the Apostles or of Holy Bishops.

Resting always on the Holy Table of every Orthodox church is a rectangular piece of cloth, about 46 by 61 centimetres (18 by 24 inches), gold in colour and folded within another larger cloth, usually but not always red in colour. The inner cloth is called the antimension and the outer the eileton, and they represent both the swaddling clothes and the burial shroud of Christ. Depicted on the top of the antimension is the Burial of Christ, together with the four Evangelists and Saints Basil the Great and John Chrysostom. Sewn into every antimension is the relic of a saint. Printed on it are the words 'By the grace of the All-Holy, Lifegiving Spirit, this Antimension, the Holy Table, is consecrated for the Offering on it of the Body and Blood of our Lord in the Divine Liturgy', with the signature of the diocesan bishop. The antimension, whose name means 'in place of a table', makes it possible to celebrate the Liturgy in places where there are no dedicated buildings, such as would be needed by missionaries and military chaplains. It must, however, be used even when the Liturgy is celebrated at a consecrated Holy Table. In addition a natural (not artificial) sponge is usually placed beside the antimension; this is used to brush off the particles from the paten into the chalice.

Beautiful hats and thigh guards

Not only is the building beautifully adorned but the clergy are also beautifully vested, though Orthodox vestments seem rather mysterious and exotic in the West. Archpriest Savely Tuberozov was given a clothbound book at his ordination in 1831 and, according to Nikolai Leskov in his novel *The Cathedral Clergy*, he used it as a journal. In it he recorded the poverty of the clergy, the progress of his marriage and the difficulty he had, as a young priest, dealing with the dissident sect of Old Believers. In 1836, having delivered an impromptu sermon in which he referred inappropriately to a living person, Tuberozov was denounced to his bishop and summoned to give an explanation for his actions. Arriving at the bishop's, he was kept waiting for thirty-six days, being fed on fish soup without the fish; then he was given the injunction that in future everything he wanted to say must be sent beforehand to the censor. He decided to give up preaching rather than submit to this bondage, but a noblewoman of his parish so admired his courage that she became his patron and benefactor, providing him with new clerical vesture – a dark brown undercassock of French silk, a cassock of green velvet and a complete set of priestly vestments. Of course, these new vestments got him into more trouble, with there being many rumours about what he had received from Lady Plodomasova. Tuberozov was again summoned by the bishop, put up in what he called 'the stink hole at the bishop's guest house', accused of various misdemeanours, placed under supervision and sent to the seminary brewhouse to brew kvass, staying from 20 January until 9 April when he was eventually allowed to go home. Lady Plodomasova again rewarded him, offering him a generous stipend for officiating three times a year in her chapel. Kvass, which is one of the national drinks of Russia, can be brewed using rye or black bread and has a low alcoholic content. It takes its colour from the bread.

Unexpectedly, given that he had actually expected to be defrocked, Tuberozov received an honour in November, when he reported, 'I have been awarded a thigh shield.' This shield, in Russian *nabédrennik*, is the first sign of distinction given to a priest. It is a rectangle of cloth with a cross at the centre that hangs down over the right thigh if worn alone or the left if the priest has been awarded the epigonation too. In February, the bishop recommended him for a calotte (*skufia*), a violet velvet cap, the second sign of distinction. The bishop was transferred to another diocese, but Tuberozov found favour with the new bishop. In August 1838, he was made an archpriest and in January 1839 received a pectoral cross. He had to wait until December 1857 to receive the *kamelaukion*, the tall brimless hat awarded as another sign of honour. The Russian *kamelaukion* or *kamilavka* is a distortion of the Greek *kalimavka*, which simply means 'beautiful hat'.

Leskov's novel reflects the uniquely Russian approach to clergy honours. Clergy wear different types of pectoral cross according to seniority, with the last, for an ordinary priest, being a gold cross. The first honour, as in Tuberozov's case, is the *nabédrennik*, which is peculiar to the Russian tradition. Before getting the gold cross, a priest will be awarded the purple *skufia* and then the purple *kamilavka*. An archpriest is invested with a special ornate pectoral cross, which may be followed by the other thigh-guard, the lozenge-shaped epigonation (Russian: *palitza*), and the pectoral jewelled cross.

Looking at the online site of a purveyor of Orthodox clerical dress it is easy to compare the Russian and Greek styles of undercassocks and overcassocks. You soon realize that Greeks and Russians use different words for the same or similar items. Included in Peter Hammond's perceptive study of the Greek Church, *The Waters of Marah*, published in 1956, is a chapter devoted to the appearance of the clergy, entitled 'Grave and different garments'. The Greek clergy were, and mostly still are, conservative in these matters. First, they are bearded. 'The notion lingers on [writes Hammond] that in the divine economy there is some mysterious connexion between the orthodoxy of an ecclesiastical personage and the length of his beard; a beardless bishop would be unthinkable.' The outdoor habit of all the Greek clergy is substantially identical. It consists of the undercassock, the inner *rason*, which is long, has narrow sleeves and is generally belted at the waist. It is called *anteri* or *zostiko* in Greek and *podryasnik* in Russian, rendered as *podrasniekka* in Finland, and is worn by all clergy under their liturgical vestments. It can be of a variety of colours: black, of course, with purple and dark blue favoured by the higher clergy, and grey, usually made from light material, also being used frequently, especially in summer. Over this is worn a fuller gown with wide sleeves. In Greek this is the *exorason* or simply the *rason*, and in Russian *riassa*. Worn over the inner cassock by clergy and monastics, it can also be worn when celebrating a service such as Vespers, but is not worn over a *sticharion*. In the Greek tradition, chanters also wear it in church, without an inner cassock.

The distinctive headgear of the Greek clergy Hammond reports as a cylinder of stiffened cloth about nine inches in height, most commonly known as the *kalymmafachion*. It is more generally rendered as *kamelavchion*. That worn by the married clergy is surmounted by a narrow brim, and the monastic form, sometimes called a *skouphos*, is brimless. The Russian version has no brim, but the diameter at the top is slightly greater than that at the bottom. Greek bishops and monastic clergy not residing in monasteries wear the type with a brim. Over these, on formal occasions including the offices in church, bishops, archimandrites and monks wear a long black veil known as the *epanokalymmafchion* or *epanokamelavchion*. It is intended to be used as the monk's shroud and is a constant reminder of death. This veil is only worn by monastic clergy. Russian metropolitans wear a white veil. A soft cap is often worn by the Greeks in monasteries, but not outdoors, while the Russians do wear the soft version when out and about.

Alas, Hammond tells us, 'it is not my intention to embark upon a detailed description of the liturgical vestments of the Greek clergy'. The problem is that pictures are needed because they are so unlike the vestments of the Latin church. He goes on to say, in a mocking tone:

> The reader who would learn to distinguish an *epigonation* from an *epitrachelion* or who would comprehend the mystical significance of the stripes of red and white which adorn an episcopal *mandyas* and are called *pomata* and *potama*, may with great profit refer to the delightful engravings which illuminate that learned writer's discussion of these matters in his work on *The Rites and Ceremonies of the Greek Church in Russia*.

The 'learned writer' was Dr John Glen King and his book, published in London in 1772, carried the explanatory subtitle '*containing an account of its Doctrine, Worship, and Discipline*'. It was a project that he began as chaplain to what was called the British Factory in St Petersburg. King's purposes were descriptive and antiquarian. King's book, with its engravings, can now be consulted online (see www.rct.uk/collection/1051871/the-rites-and-ceremonies-of-the-greek-church-in-russia). The glossary to this book contains descriptions of Orthodox eucharistic vestments.

Figure 1 **The Holy Table during the Liturgy**

Figure 2 **The prosphoron (Greek style)**

Figure 3 **The priest, Father Alexander, in full vestments, prepares the consecrated bread that is to be added to the wine in the chalice for communion for the people**

Figure 4 **A typical Russian-style church (Kuopio, Finland)**

Figure 5 **Father Nikolai, in full vestments with a jewelled pectoral cross, blesses the water**

Figure 6 **The sprinkling of the people after the blessing of the water**

Figure 7 **The Great Entry on Great and Holy Saturday morning**

Figure 8 **Bishop and senior priest before the altar at Sourozh Cathedral, London. As it is not a hierarchical (that is, pontifical) Liturgy, the bishop wears the phelonion rather than the sakkos. His crozier, with veil, stands to the right of the Holy Doors.**

Figure 9 **Archbishop Theophanes of the Jerusalem Patriarchate in his formal outdoor clothes with panagia and holding the episcopal walking stick**

5

The holy icons

On the Sunday of Orthodoxy, the Church professes its faith in the Holy Trinity in this form:

> We know one Lord and God,
> glorified in three Persons,
> and Him alone we worship;
> we have one faith, one baptism,
> and we are clothed in Christ.
> This is our salvation
> we confess in deed and word,
> and we depict it in the holy icons.

We have seen that the iconoclast heresy left a lasting scar on the Orthodox Church. Today there may be argument about the style of icons, but there is none about their significance as objects of devotion. What is an icon? The word itself derives directly from the ancient Greek word *eikon*, meaning likeness, image and representation. The Greek dimension is significant. The great scholar Steven Runciman, writing of the fall of Constantinople in 1453 and reviewing the city's legacy, wrote with characteristic insight that its rulers down the centuries

> had inspired and encouraged a school of art unparalleled in human history, an art that arose from an ever varying blend of the cool cerebral Greek sense of the fitness of things and a deep religious sense that saw in works of art the incarnation of the Divine and the sanctification of matter.

American art historian and Byzantine specialist Anna Kartsonis affirms icons as among the most potent expressions of the culture of Byzantium, the supreme visual statements of its religiosity, spirituality and piety. They are one of the answers Byzantium provides to the universal problem of human existence and to the desire to access and participate in the realm of the divine. In terms of the Orthodox ethos as defined here, icons can be located within the categories of boundary, beauty, biography and miracle.

Icons abound in the churches of the Orthodox tradition. Indeed, the Orthodox Church is inconceivable without icons, lit candles and burning incense. Equally, for an icon to exist *as an icon* rather than as a work of art, it must be placed within the context of prayer. Wood and paint and varnish and glass, the printed image, the photographic image, can all have multiple uses. They are a part of the material world. Much modern art is dissonant, shocking in intention and consequence, but the essence of the combination made in an icon is beauty, harmony, unity and joy. It represents life as God intended it to be, life that is not disrupted by ugliness, division, alienation, misery and death. The icon represents and makes present the new creation in Jesus Christ. The icon in its unity and simplicity shows us the redeemed state. Looking at an icon is like looking into a glass that does much more than reflect our image; it shows what we are and what we could be. It does not show fame or fortune or power, but reveals the state of holiness, the glorified state. Like something that shows a person at ideal weight and body mass, looking at an icon may be disconcerting. Standing before it and seeing it for what it is – a participation in God – may make one realize the significance of human brokenness and alienation from God. Contemplation of an icon may require penitence, the repentance that leads us from self-destruction to life. It can move the beholder to a state between sorrow and joy. The inner light of the icon exposes the inner darkness of the soul, but the light is a healing and purifying light. It is said that looking at a good icon, contemplating it, inspires prayer. When one can at last pray – and the movement towards prayer may be hindered by our worldly concerns – when prayerfulness is achieved, it is possible to become still and attentive, attuned and peaceful, entering into communion with the icon's source, with its prototype.

An icon can be a commodity. An icon in a church was probably commissioned, then created, exported perhaps, invoiced and paid for. One might look and see a painting on wood, perhaps by a Greek artist, painted in Greece, or by a Russian painted in Russia. One may say, 'I like it' or 'It doesn't do anything for me.' It is possible to say, 'I prefer this icon to that one' and to do so would be to treat it precisely as a commodity. If one looks at it differently, and it takes time and practice to do so, then where it was made and who painted it for how much becomes irrelevant. It is now seen as a religious item and its veneration as a religious act. It might help those who look to see themselves as they are – not in terms of bones and muscles and blood and major and minor organs, but as created and sustained by God, redeemed by Christ, and destined for glory – nothing ordinary and definitely not a commodity. That too takes time and practice, to see ourselves and other people as seen by the all-seeing loving eye of God.

This is a lot to ask of a picture, a painting, a print or photograph, but really it is what the icon asks of the one who looks at it, who contemplates it. Looking at an icon, the viewer can describe the scene, decide whether the icon is from this place or that, this period or that, historic or modern, Greek or Russian or Romanian. It is possible to talk of the method of painting, the sequence of colours, the stylized figures and so on, but all that is really irrelevant. The icon is a religious artefact; a devotional item with a purpose. Using the language of Platonic philosophy, it participates in its form and invites the viewer to join in that participation. It may be primitive or sophisticated in its form, but it is truly an icon if it makes that connection. If it does not, it is only a picture. The true icon demands much of the person who looks at it.

In a broader sense, the word 'icon' can refer to a living image, a reflected image, an imaginary form, a phantom, an image in the mind, and to something that represents some greater reality (as it does on the computer screen). When we refer to an icon in a religious sense, and in a specifically Orthodox sense, we are referring to images with religious meaning painted on panels and generally depicting Christ, the Theotokos, angels, Apostles and other saints, as well as narrative scenes from their lives. Icons range in size from larger-than-life-size to pocket-size. They can be made of wood and paint, mosaic, ivory, silver, gold and enamel, and today might well be photographic images of existing icons mounted on wood or card or plastic or even self-printed on paper. They may be one-off or mass-produced. They are often portable, though they might be painted directly on to the walls of a church. Many Orthodox churches have large numbers of icons on the walls, some on special stands, perhaps beneath a baldacchino or canopy, and a large group on the screen separating the sanctuary from the rest of the church and known for that reason as the iconostasis. On the screen, the larger icons are placed on each side of the central doors and smaller icons are placed higher up; there are icons on the doors themselves and on the lintels.

Kartsonis explains that size, shape, form, subject matter, medium and setting do not suffice to define or make an icon; this is done by two relationships, that of the image to its prototype and that of the person represented (the image) to the viewer. In religious terms one does not view an icon as one might look at pictures in a gallery. The act of viewing and kissing, preceded by prostrations, is termed 'venerating'. St John of Damascus said that this veneration is not offered to matter, but to those who are portrayed through matter in the images. Writing about the theology of the icon, icon painter Mariamna Fortounatto and theologian Mary B. Cunningham call icons confessions of faith, witnesses to the Incarnation, and symbols manifesting something greater than the physical limits allow. Icons offer 'a window into eternal meaning' and as such are worthy of honour and devotion. They also describe the icon as a microcosm, a mediator of divine reality, linking the divine and created worlds, acting as a window or passageway between human beings and God. We can say, therefore, that they act as boundary points, marking not the limit of movement, as would a wall or a border fence, but a frontier, the crossing point, a crossing they themselves facilitate.

Icons may be best understood both by looking at them and by attending to their stories, many of which are about the making of icons and many of which involve miracle. In a serendipitous survey spanning Constantinople, Athos, Kiev, Volokolamsk and Valamo, we can see how Orthodox icons are connected and see also that, like the saints, an icon can have a biography. There are actually surprisingly few mentions of icons in Byzantine lives of saints. There is an interesting example in the life of Athanasios of Athos (version B), dated between 1050 and 1150. Antony, who became the superior of the Panagiou monastery in Constantinople, was a close disciple of Athanasios. After his death, a monk named Kosmas, coming from Athos to visit Antony, saw in his possession an icon of 'the great father', Athanasios, which is described as 'a perfect likeness of his holy appearance'. He asked to be given it. Antony, understandably, refused the request saying that he couldn't possibly be totally deprived of the icon. After some wrangling he agreed, however, that it could be copied in three days, saying 'we may use this archetype to make another icon'. Around the time of the Mattins hymns, Antony went to Pantoleon the icon-maker, explained the matter to him and urged him not to be slow about making the copy. Pantaleon could not understand why Antony had come himself, as his disciple had come late the previous day to inform him of the matter and he had not only made all the preparations but was about to start painting. After investigation, it became clear that Athanasios himself had been the emissary. Within three days the copy was finished and Kosmas took the original to the holy Lavra on Athos, where it was placed beside the tomb of Athanasios and was much venerated, 'since it preserves the precise features of his holy appearance'. The Byzantines did not consider a copy in the least inferior to an original and didn't differentiate them. The essential nature of the archetype passed into the copy, and a copy of a wonder-working icon was likely itself to be wonder-working.

At the Kiev Pechersky monastery, as the *Paterikon* relates, St Theodosius moved out of the caves where St Anthony had started his brotherhood and, together with the brothers, built a large wooden church which was then decorated with icons. This was

followed in due course by a new stone church. The master craftsmen who came from Constantinople to direct the building had
been sent, they said, by 'the Empress'. They were unaware that
the noblewoman who appeared to them was the Theotokos, and
they brought to Kiev a special wonder-working icon of her to place
on the iconostasis. Icons of this sort, described as not made with
hands, *acheiropoieton*, are a very important part of Orthodox tradition. There is a further such occurrence in Kiev. After St Anthony
and St Theodosius reposed, icon painters in Constantinople saw the
two saints together in a vision and were instructed by them to proceed to Kiev, though they only discovered who they were when they
saw portraits at the monastery. They encountered many difficulties on the journey and thought of returning home, but saw an icon
of the Most Holy Theotokos in a dream and heard a voice ordering them to continue the journey. We are told they then adorned
the entire monastery with holy icons. The Greek painters took on St
Alipius as their apprentice, and after they left his iconographic skills
continued to develop. He painted icons free for anyone who asked
and was never idle. Any money he received he divided into three
equal parts: for buying materials, for the poor and for the needs
of the monastery. He maintained an ascetic life and was ordained
to the priesthood, and became known for his wonder-working.
Some monks took some silver and seven large icon boards from a
man who wanted Alipius to decorate a new church in Kiev. They
never told St Alipius, but told the man that he needed more silver.
Eventually, having not received the icons, the man complained to
the abbot. On being questioned, St Alipius said, 'I do not know
what you are talking about.' The abbot sent for the unpainted icon
boards that had been seen the day before in a storeroom. Monks
went to fetch them and found, instead of plain boards, seven beautifully painted icons. The unjust monks were found out yet did not
repent. The icons were installed, but the church where they were
kept burned down during a major fire in Kiev. Despite this, the
icons were found to be completely unharmed. Prince Vladimir
Monomakh, hearing of the miracles, sent the icon of the Theotokos
to a new stone church in Rostov on Don, and it was miraculously

preserved on two further occasions. In St Alipius's old age, when he was too sick to paint an icon of the Dormition, an angel painted a shining icon and took it to the church for which it was intended, returning to take the saint's soul. The conclusion of the account of St Alipius briefly expresses the Orthodox theology of the image:

> Thus, the holy wonderworking icon painter adorned heaven and earth, honouring the Icon painter–creator, God the Father, Who said, *Let us make man in Our image, after Our likeness* and the image of His Incarnation, God the Son, Who took on the Image Himself together with the Holy Spirit Who came down in the image of a dove and of fiery tongues.

In this way, the theology of the icon is grounded on God who created humankind in the divine image and likeness, on the Son who, in the Incarnation, took on the divine image found in humanity and was doubly the image of the Father and the Spirit, who, though invisible, was manifest as a dove and as fire.

Among those things on which we are informed incidentally by the monastic paterika is the reverence given to icons and the use made of them. There are a number of such examples in the *Volokolamsk Paterikon*. A man who prayed to the Megalomartyr Nikita for healing saw him on a horse in a vision and subsequently went to the Dormition Cathedral in Moscow to give thanks, asking where the saint's icon (meaning, it seems, an image on the wall, not a portable icon) was painted. One of the uses of icons was indeed to enable believers who had dreams of saints to identify them. Conversely, if a saint's name was mentioned in a dream the dreamer would seek out the icon to identify the saint, as we saw with the woman who was asked to bring a walking stick to church by the hitherto unknown St Gerasimos. At Volokolamsk monastery, which was dedicated to the Most Pure Theotokos, a monk was found in his cell, kneeling in prayer 'before God's icon and the icon of the Most Pure Theotokos', holding his prayer beads and with tears on his face, in which posture he had died. We see too a sick room where a woman who regains some strength raises herself up and, supported by two other women, kisses an icon of the Dormition. There are icons painted by the famous Andrej Rublev (1360/70– c. 1430) and the monastic icon painter Dionisj that are sent as gifts to bribe or appease the local prince. The Hegumen sends a respected elder to see the angry archbishop of Novgorod and he goes carrying an icon of the Theotokos, apparently as a form of protection. A monk, Kassian, has a special devotion to an icon described as being 'of the Most Pure Theotokos, who held in her arms the Creator of the world, the Pre-eternal Child'. He can gaze on it from his bed. It is to this same icon that he turns when the refectory roof has caught fire and the monks' cells are starting to burn, saying, 'Most Pure, Most Pure, you have loved this place! Fend off this punishment by your mercy,' and the flames are immediately blown a different way and burn themselves out.

Icons are like people in having a story, a biography that may go from creation to destruction and that often involves travels and adventures. In addition to a nineteenth-century wonder-working icon of Our Lady of Valamo, mentioned earlier, there are two other icons from Valamo monastery worthy of note. The first is the All-Holy Virgin of the Sign. The remote prototype of icons of this sort was honoured in the church in the quarter of Blachernai in Constantinople, built around 457. It gave its name to icons depicting the Mother of God with arms raised in prayer and a small figure of Christ depicted in an aureole in the centre of her chest; the title was *Blachernaitissa*. The four master craftsmen sent to Kiev had been called to a meeting with the empress at Blachernai and it might be assumed that the icon they were given was of this sort. Later, in Russia, these icons were given the name *Znamenie*, meaning 'a sign'. A nineteenth-century note on the one at Valamo says, 'It is unknown when this very old holy icon came to this monastery.' The *riza* – a metal cover on an icon, which covers all or part of it except the faces and other exposed areas, such as hands and feet – was made in 1804. It was Hegumen Innokenty who, on a visit to Novgorod, noted that the Valamo icon appeared to be a free copy of one that he saw there, the wonder-working icon of the Virgin of the Sign. This icon-palladium (protective image) is a two-sided processional icon, with a portrayal of the Saviour with Peter and Natalia the Martyr standing before Him on the reverse. It was made in the first half of the twelfth century. According to a fourteenth-century legend, this icon saved Novgorod in 1170 from the besieging troops of the Suzdalian prince Andrei Bogolyubsky. After prayer before the icon, it was taken out to the fortified wall to be shown to the enemy. There it was hit by arrows and tears flowed from it. The chronicle declares:

> O, great awe-inspiring miracle! How may it be from a dry wood? These are not tears, but She showed a token of Her grace: that is the way in which Our Lady was praying to Her Son and our God for our city not to be forsaken for the adversaries to outrage it.

The Novgorod icon resembled the Mother of God of Blachernai and was henceforth called by the name *Znameni*, meaning 'sign', but also 'miracle', 'symbol', 'image' and even 'war standard'. The old Novgorod icon was restored in the sixteenth century, which changed its appearance somewhat, making it less bright. It is the obverse only of this version, the image of the Theotokos, that was copied, probably in the seventeenth century, for Valamo. It was incorporated into the upper tier of icons on the main tier of the iconostasis of the old upper church of the Transfiguration at old Valamo monastery in 1848. It was renovated in 1892 by the monk Alipi, who must surely have already been an icon painter when he was tonsured and so was given the name of St Alipius of Kiev Pechersky, and was placed over the shrine of Saints Sergei and Herman in the new lower church. From there it was taken to New Valamo during the Winter War of 1939–1940. As it was in a poor state of repair, a reconstructed copy was made in 1994, using the Valamo version and its immediate prototype together with Novgorodian icons from the sixteenth and seventeenth centuries to recreate its original appearance. Another Russian double-sided icon, of the Mother of God of Blachernai, in the National Museum of Finland, may well have begun as a copy of the

Novgorod prototype, but with the Archangel Michael on the reverse. This icon seems to have been painted for soldiers who served in the Russian army in the Crimean War and it made its way on the steamship *Suomi* (Finland), which had served in the Russian navy during the war from Crimea to Finland. Each copy adds a new layer of meaning.

Another Valamo icon is older and has a more complex history. It came to New Valamo from the monastery of Konevitsa. St Arseni, who died in 1447, was the founder of that monastery. He was born into a Christian family in Novgorod, trained as a coppersmith and entered a monastery. He went to Mount Athos, and after staying there for three years resolved to return to Russia to found a monastery dedicated to the Nativity of the Mother of God. On his departure he was given an icon of the Mother of God of the Dove, known on Athos as 'of the Athonite Acathistos'. The monastery was founded on the island of Konevitsa in Lake Ladoga in 1393 and the icon's miracle-working properties were soon recognized by the monks. Various disasters befell the monks. The church burned down in Easter week 1553, but the icon was saved. The monastery was sacked in 1580 during the Russo-Swedish War and the monks fled to the monastery of Derevyanitsa in Novgorod with all their portable goods. They returned to the rebuilt monastery in 1598 and Boris Godunov presented a silk-embroidered cloth for the icon. The monks were forced out again in the seventeenth century, taking refuge first at Derevyanitsa, then at Tikhon and then again at Derevyanitsa. Writing to the Tsar in 1717 with a request that monastic life at Konevitsa should recommence, Archimandrite Yoanniki said that they had been in exile since 1610 and still had with them the icon that Arseni brought back from Athos. The icon, as was quite common with wonder-working icons, was taken on a three-month visit to St Petersburg and a number of healing miracles took place among those who came to venerate it. Some merchants from the capital provided the icon with a *riza* in 1798 when it was first known as 'the Icon of the Mother of God of Konevitsa'. When the island monastery was evacuated in 1939–1940, the monks took the icon first to Hiekka in Keitele and then, as their numbers diminished, to New Valamo. Hence a fourteenth-century icon from Athos is today venerated by the Orthodox in Finland.

The Orthodox certainly believed in the intercessory power of significant icons and the rites associated with them, and Constantinople contained many icons that were considered as symbols of the city with powers that might be protective. The icons were, however, not bound to work miracles and were not considered as magical. They were certainly thought, on the basis of experience, to be more effective than other icons in opening the boundary, but its permeability depended both on the faith and virtue of those praying and, crucially, on the will of God. Even with such palladium-icons failure, famine, disease and defeat were possible. The best example of this is an icon, said to have been painted by St Luke, associated with the defeat of iconoclasm. It is that of the Theotokos known as Hodegetria, from the monastery church of Hodegos which was said to have been built by the Emperor Michael III after the definitive restoration of the icons in 843. It was this icon that was taken through the streets of the imperial city in procession on Tuesdays. On the Thursday before Palm Sunday it was taken to the Imperial Palace to join another icon of the Virgin which had its own chapel there, the *Nikopoia* (literally 'the victory-maker', which might be the one that is venerated in a chapel in San Marco in Venice). The Hodegetria returned to her own church on Bright Monday. In 1453 during the siege of Constantinople the icon of the Theotokos Hodegetria was taken to the church of the monastery of the Holy Saviour in Chora that she might inspire the defenders of the walls and protect the city. Steven Runciman tells that a procession took place in the besieged city but, as the icon was moved slowly through the streets, it suddenly slipped from its platform. Those who rushed to raise it said it was as heavy as if it were made of lead. With much effort it was remounted, but then a dreadful thunderstorm burst on the city, flooding the streets, and the procession was abandoned. These events combined with others seemed to be omens pointing to the fall of the city. Having breached the walls on 29 May 1453 and with the city given over to three days of looting, the invaders found the precious icon in Chora as they stripped the churches of plate, vestments and anything else of value. It is told that four Turks quarrelled over the icon; it was torn from its setting and hacked into four pieces.

The destruction of icons was also a feature of the Russian Revolution. Icon painting declined in Russia between the seventeenth century and the mid-nineteenth century, with strong Western influences that were alien to the Byzantine and Russian traditions. As the economy grew markedly in the nineteenth century, new churches were built. Under the influence of saintly Bishop Brianchaninov and others, there was a return to more traditional icon painting, especially in the St Petersburg studio of Vasili Makarovich Peshekhonov, icon painter to the Imperial Court. The influence of Byzantium was again apparent as icon painters used Byzantine and ancient Russian prototypes and also sought advice from Old Believers, the schismatics (*Raskol*) who were nonetheless experts on historic icons. Their strong relationship to their icons and knowledge of icon painting is well illustrated in Nikolai Leskov's story 'The Sealed Angel' (1873). This movement in icon painting, which recovered styles from before the seventeenth-century schism, was matched in music by the increased use of historic Russian chant. The Peshekhonov icons have been described as always harmonious and of a carefully considered composition based on texts from the Gospels and the Liturgy and on ancient iconographic traditions. It was these icons that perished in huge numbers as the Bolsheviks closed down and demolished churches or converted them to new secular uses. Those that have survived are mostly in Finland and form a unique collection that demonstrates the understanding of the icon as 'an element of theology expressed in colours' reflecting pre-Revolutionary Russian Orthodox spirituality.

The restoration of the Church after the fall of the Soviet Union has led to iconographic innovation. The major force behind this is the canonization of the new martyrs and confessors of Russia – those who were killed or suffered arrest and deprivation under the Bolsheviks – all of whom need icons or at least to be included in collective icons. We saw that the monk Kosmas wanted the icon of Athanasios because it preserved the precise features of his holy appearance. The question for contemporary iconographers was the degree to which the icon of someone should resemble family photographs or the 'mug shots' taken in the Gulag, given that it was to convey the spiritual essence of the new saint and to fulfil its primary devotional purpose. The tradition of icon painting offers some guidance because the icon represents the person depicted without being equated with its model, like a photograph, and older icons were used as types. The icon painter is not imitating the type, but creating a new icon on the basis of a prototype, using a similar saint, a confessor or a martyr, for example, to create both a new icon and a new prototype.

How should the icon be used in prayer? Orthodox Christians will generally own many icons, while having a particular attachment to certain ones. Church shops, especially those at Russian monasteries, sell a vast number of small, affordable icons, very often with the saint's name and troparion printed on the reverse. People will wear them, carry them, have them in their cars and their homes, often though not always in an icon, or beautiful, corner with an oil lampada and an incense burner. They may say their daily prayers in front of their household icons and address the saint represented there. In church, they are somewhat less likely to focus on one icon but, on arrival and departure, venerate many, starting, in a Russian church, with the icon of the feast or of the Resurrection on the central analoy, before going to those of Christ and the Theotokos and the patron saint, then visiting other icons. Yet they cannot be said to be using an icon to pray. There are books to be found with titles such as *How to Pray with Icons* but they are never by Orthodox writers; two popular ones are by former Archbishop of Canterbury Rowan Williams and the Roman Catholic spiritual writer Henri Nouwen. Such books certainly encourage people to look at icons as more than works of art and to understand more about the Christian faith, and especially about Christ, the Theotokos and the saints, by apprehending them in a visual way, but guidance on prayer by Orthodox writers never, in my experience, refers to icons. The distinguished British Orthodox priest and theologian Andrew Louth once responded to the question 'How should I pray with an icon?' by saying something along the lines of 'Stand before it and *close your eyes.*' Metropolitan Kallistos Ware, writing about the Jesus Prayer, said that it is normally recited in complete darkness or with the eyes closed, 'not with open eyes before an icon illuminated by candles or a votive lamp'. Russian theologian Sergius Bulgakov stressed that the correct relationship between the iconic image and its Prototype had to be maintained to ensure that the icon did not become, on the one hand, a mere religious picture, of a subjective anthropomorphic kind, and, on the other hand, a fetish, by which he means a thing that is regarded as the habitation of God and is identified with Him (which would make it both fetish and idol). Bulgakov says that no matter how high a value one places on the icon, its significance is limited. He is clear both that it serves as a place for the meeting in prayer with God and that the intermediary of the icon is not a necessary condition for prayer. Prayer is possible without icons, which, however, belong to the fullness of Christian truth. To assert that prayer is impossible without icons would also be a kind of fetishism and idolatry.

So, if it is not to be a sort of transmitter required for prayer, what is the purpose of the icon today? To understand that we need to go back to the question of what makes a person Orthodox, in the sense (using the words of anthropologist Vlad Naumescu) of what enables an individual to grow 'into a faith that weaves its teachings into a rich spiritual tradition, theology and practice'. 'Being Orthodox' always means 'becoming Orthodox' in the sense of the process of becoming what you already are, a process that does not end until you repose. The images of the saints are important in this, and especially for the Orthodox-born. Even if they give up Christian practice and become secular, as many do, they continue to be moved by the embodied experience that shaped them initially, especially the familiar and distinctive smell of 'church' and the saints who look back at you from the icons. Orthodoxy does not prescribe any single path towards the formation of Christian personhood but, rather, encourages people to search for their own way. The guides will include the parish priest, other priests, monks and nuns, those encountered on pilgrimage, among whom may be some 'elders', as well as spiritual

writers, who are mostly the elders of past ages, and the moral exemplars (re)presented in the icons. The saints are holy figures who are
powerful intercessors and exemplars of ethical virtues. Naumescu
points to three qualities of icons. First, they are ideal illustrations of
this exemplarity grounding a relational ethics. Relational ethics is
a contemporary approach to ethics that situates ethical action explicitly in relationship. If ethics is about how we should live, then it
is essentially about how we should live together, and it has proved
to be a fruitful approach for those involved in the caring professions, especially nurses. Second, icons are spiritualized portrayals
of concrete human persons who were changed (transfigured) by
their experience of God. Third, those (re)presented in icons guide
and instruct believers, inviting them to imitate their *virtues* rather
than the *person*. Holy icons join holy relics and the lives of saints
to create interactive foci of saintly presence. Having venerated the
relics of a saint (which I cannot generally take home with me), and
having bought an icon (which I can), I read and re-read the life (in a
book or online) and pray to and through the saint, asking the saint
to pray for me. In addition I try, in this active relationship, to emulate the virtues exemplified by my saint (as he or she has become).
Leonid Ouspensky, one of the greatest iconographers and iconolo-
gists of the twentieth century, author of the two-volume classic text
Theology of the Icon, summarizes it in this way:

> By word and by image, the liturgy sanctifies our senses. Being
> an expression of the image and likeness of God restored in
> man, the icon is a dynamic and constructive element of
> worship. This is why the church, by the decision of the seventh
> ecumenical council, orders that icons be placed 'on the same
> level as the images of the life-giving cross, in all of the churches
> of God, on vases [vessels] and sacred vestments, on the walls,
> on wooden boards, in homes and in the streets.

In the icon, the church recognizes one of the means which can and
must allow us to realize our calling, that is, to attain the likeness
of our divine prototype, to accomplish in our life that which is

revealed and transmitted to us by the God-man. The saints are very few in number, but holiness is a task assigned to all, and icons are placed everywhere to serve as examples of holiness, as a revelation of the holiness of the world to come, a plan and a project of the cosmic transfiguration. Furthermore, since the grace attained by the saints during their lives continues to dwell in their images, these images are placed everywhere for the sanctification of the world by the grace which belongs to them. Icons are like the markers on our path to the new creation, so that, according to Paul, in contemplating 'the glory of the Lord, [we] are being changed into his likeness' (2 Corinthians 3.18).

6

The Holy Liturgy

There are three liturgies in use in the Orthodox Church: St John Chrysostom, St Basil and the Presanctified. The last of these is used on Wednesdays and Fridays in Lent and on the Monday, Tuesday and Wednesday of Holy Week. The Liturgy of St Basil, somewhat longer than that of St John Chrysostom, is celebrated on all Sundays in Lent except Palm Sunday, on Maundy Thursday, the Saturday of Holy Week, the Vigils of Christmas and Epiphany, and on the feast of St Basil (1 January). The Divine Liturgy of Our Father among the Saints John Chrysostom is the normal Liturgy and an account of it will be given here.

The temple with its icons, as we have described it, is the essential context and background to the Liturgy, an apparently empty space that needs to be populated. Arriving early for a service, one might witness the awakening of the building – the correct icon being put in place on the central analoy and the changing of cloths to the appropriate colour, the lighting of lamps, the placing of flower vases, the cleaning of the glass of icons, the sorting and setting out of music, the removal to storage of vestments worn on a previous day. Someone will already be at the candle stall ready to receive the lists of prayers for the living and the dead. Bells may be ringing. The Holy Doors of the iconostasis are closed and the curtain, if there is one, is closed. The oil lamp that burns in front of the icon of the Last Supper has been lowered; it will be lit, but only raised when the Liturgy is about to begin. New arrivals will hang up coats, stow bags, buy a handful of candles and proceed to venerate the festal icon and those of Christ, the Most Holy Theotokos, the temple's patron and others that are special to them, and any relics of saints displayed in the temple, lighting their candles, murmuring short prayers and then finding a place to stand, often waiting to make confession. Though the faithful may greet friends and family, in a Russian church at least this is a quite secondary matter. As lamps and candles illumine the icons, there is a recognition that this is not, and never has been, an empty space, but one always standing ready to worship the Holy Trinity. When the priest arrives, already in his cassock, he too will venerate the icons in the nave or naos and those of the iconostasis, and any relics. Then, passing through one of the Deacon's Doors into the sanctuary, he will go to put on his epitrachelion. Having bowed profoundly and three times to the Holy Table and kissed the edge of it, he will go, with the deacon, to stand before the Holy Doors and begin the entry prayers. (Some churches do not have a deacon and there are sometimes several priests with the senior performing some of the diaconal functions; in this description it will be assumed that there is a deacon.) At the conclusion the clergy bow to one another and then to the people, asking for forgiveness, before entering again into the sanctuary.

There will soon be many things going on. The chanter or reader may begin the Third Hour followed by the Sixth, servers may arrive and seek a blessing before putting on a sticharion, and one of the priests may take his place to hear confessions prior to the Liturgy. Although the priest, unseen in the sanctuary, will be occupied with the Proskomide, he is still heard making the necessary conclusions to the prayers of the reader. The entry prayers completed, the clergy will vest for the Eucharist. Blessed by the priest, the deacon takes the sticharion and orarion. Saying the vesting prayers, they both put on their vestments. The priest takes his and puts them on in the order sticharion, epitrachelion, girdle (zone), right cuff, left cuff, epigo-nation, phelonion and pectoral cross. They wash their hands and then go to the Prothesis, to the Table of Oblation, to begin the Rite of Preparation. With the prosphora in his left hand and the Holy Lance in his right, and reciting words from Isaiah 53 that identify Christ as a sheep led to the slaughter and as the Lamb of God, tak-ing away the sin of the world, the priest, in the words of the rubrics, thrusts the Lance into the prosphora as the deacon says, 'Sacrifice, Master'. From the prosphora will be taken the large portion, which is known as the Lamb, and it is placed on the paten. It is the part of the loaf that is stamped with the monogram IC XP above and NI KA below, and it is the only part that will be consecrated. Then the priest will put wine and water into the chalice, after which a number of particles, representative of the Theotokos, the saints, the bishops and those to be prayed for, the living and the dead, will be taken from other prosphora and be arranged in a quite deliberate fashion with the Lamb on the paten. These portions will be put into the chalice before the communion of the people. Incense is blessed and the asterisk (the star) is placed on the paten over the holy bread. The first veil is censed and the paten and asterisk are covered. The second veil is censed and placed over the chalice and then the aër too is censed and placed over both paten and chalice. The priest, in the Offertory Prayer, asks God to 'bless this Offering, and receive it on your altar above the heavens'. The Rite of Preparation ends with the deacon censing the Prothesis. The curtain is opened and the lamp raised. The deacon censes the Holy Table and the whole sanctuary before going out of the Deacon's Doors to cense the Holy Doors, the icons of the screen and the other icons. This appearance of the deacon, heralded by the sound of the bells on the censer from within the sanctuary, may be the first thing that is seen by the people standing in the nave, who move away from the sides to enable the deacon to cense the icons on the walls, standing with bowed head as he censes them too. It is important to understand that the Prothesis is at least notionally a place separate from the sanctuary for during the Great Entrance the Holy Gifts will be ritually brought to the Holy Table and not merely transferred from one table to another within the sanctuary. In the same way historically the first part of the Liturgy itself preceded the coming of the clergy to the sanctuary, and whereas now they come out of one door of the sanctuary shortly to return by another, the significance of what is being done is much greater (and in some churches the processions do come the long way, passing through the nave before returning). The Greek and Russian liturgies both, of course, have the Rite of Preparation, but the Greeks usually have Orthros (Mattins) sung before the Liturgy, ending with the Great Doxology and the troparion of the Sunday. The Russians will have sung the Great Doxology during the All-Night Vigil (see Chapter 7).

Space simply does not allow for a lengthy description of the whole Liturgy. It would, anyway, be as complex and difficult as trying to describe a performance (any performance, but especially opera) that involves an interaction of words, music and actions. Added to those elements, for the Liturgy, are the outer (physical) and inner (spiritual and emotional) responses of the faithful. It is nearly impossible to describe, for example, what it is like in a church at the moment when the priest says Christ's words over the Lamb, the bread on the paten, together with the wine in the chalice, the triple 'Amen' being said after the words 'changing them by your Holy Spirit' and the whole congregation, though standing close together, silently and seemingly easily prostrating in veneration. The Divine Liturgy has to be devoutly experienced and in that experience one might begin to grasp what Mother Thekla meant by the Orthodox paradox that is carried into worship and which she expressed in the words already quoted, 'We know because we believe and we believe because we know.' Nevertheless, it is helpful to understand the structure of the Liturgy, which will now be set out.

The Divine Liturgy of Our Father among the Saints John Chrysostom divides into three parts: the Prothesis, which we have already described; the Liturgy of the Catechumens (so-called because those preparing for Baptism were allowed to be present at it); and the Liturgy of the Faithful. The catechumens were dismissed before the Great Entrance and so did not hear the Creed or witness the offering of the Holy Mysteries. The deacon, having returned with the censer to the sanctuary, completes the censing of the Holy Table and after asking for a blessing goes by way of the north door to stand before the Holy Doors, beginning, 'Master, give the blessing.' The priest says, 'Blessed is the Kingdom of the Father, and of the Son, and of the Holy Spirit, now and ever, and to the ages of ages' and the choir sings 'Amen'. The deacon then begins the Litany of Peace, standing before the doors and holding up his orarion with three fingers of his right hand. The choir responds, 'Lord, have mercy' to each petition and the litany concludes with the words, 'Commemorating our most holy, pure, blessed and glorified Lady, Mother of God and Ever-Virgin Mary, with all the Saints, let us commend ourselves and one another and our whole life to Christ, our God.'

The next part of the service consists of three Antiphons, with prayers said quietly by the priest, each followed by a versicle and response and the Little Litany, which begins, 'Again and again . . .' and includes the last petition of the Great Litany. After the Antiphons, the Little Entrance takes place. The ministers, preceded by one or two candle-bearers, pass through the Prothesis out to the front of the iconostasis by way of the north door, carrying the Book of the Gospels. Before the open Holy Doors the deacon will raise the book and say, 'Wisdom. Stand upright,' then priest and deacon will enter the sanctuary and place the Gospel Book on the Holy Table, while the candle-bearers remain outside. The priest kisses the icons on the right and left of the doors and, turning from the one to the other, blesses and dismisses the candle-bearers. The choir sings the Entrance Chant followed by the Trisagion ('Holy God, Holy and Mighty, Holy and Immortal, have mercy on us'). The people are standing attentively throughout this, crossing themselves and bowing or bowing their heads at appropriate moments.

The Epistle, known in Orthodox liturgy as the Apostle, is read by a reader, the deacon having first said, 'Wisdom' and, 'Let us attend.' There is a chant, the Prokeimenon, by the reader and the choir. There is often a censing at this point, a distraction to reader and hearers, which should be properly done during the following Alleluia, now sung by the choir while the deacon is blessed. Before the Gospel it is the priest who says, 'Wisdom. Stand upright,' followed by, 'Let us listen to the Holy Gospel. Peace to all.' The Gospel is announced and chanted. The deacon returns the book to the priest and 'standing in his usual place' (as the rubric says) begins the Litany of Fervent Supplication, characterized by its triple 'Lord, have mercy' for each petition other than the first two. The Litany for the Catechumens, having fallen out of use for a time, is again being said; it ends with the insistent instruction given by the deacon, 'As many as are catechumens, depart; catechumens, depart; as many as are catechumens, depart. Let none of the catechumens remain.' Meanwhile, the priest has unfolded the antimension and spread it on the Holy Table.

Now the Liturgy of the Faithful begins, with the words of the deacon, 'As many as are of the faithful, again and again in peace, let us pray to the Lord,' and two short litanies in succession. The Great Entrance now takes place, bringing the prepared bread and wine from the Prothesis to the Holy Table and this is done with all possible solemnity. As the procession is being marshalled, the choir begins the Cherubic Hymn, as follows: 'We, who mystically represent the Cherubim, sing the thrice-holy hymn to the life-giving Trinity. Let us put away all earthly care, so that we may receive the King of All, invisibly escorted by the Angelic Hosts. Alleluia.' At the words 'King of All', the choir pauses and the procession takes place. Various biddings are made, praying for the patriarch, bishops, other clergy, the civil authorities and so on, differing in the various jurisdictions but generally ending with a petition that God may remember in His Kingdom 'all of you Orthodox Christians'. The choir finishes the Cherubic Hymn when the clergy have entered the sanctuary and the Holy Gifts are laid on the Holy Table. The deacon returns to his usual place for the Litany of the Precious Gifts, one of the loveliest litanies in the Liturgy. Here is part of it:

Deacon: Help us, save us, have mercy on us, and keep us, O God, by Thy grace.
Choir: Lord, have mercy.
Deacon: That the whole day may be perfect, holy, peaceful, and sinless, let us ask of the Lord.
Choir: Grant this, O Lord.
Deacon: An angel of peace, a faithful guide, a guardian of our souls and bodies, let us ask of the Lord.
Choir: Grant this, O Lord.
Deacon: Pardon and remission of our sins and offences, let us ask of the Lord.

Choir: Grant this, O Lord.

Deacon: Things good and profitable for our souls, and peace for the world, let us ask of the Lord.

Choir: Grant this, O Lord.

Deacon: That we may complete the remaining time of our life in peace and repentance, let us ask of the Lord.

Choir: Grant this, O Lord.

Deacon: A Christian ending to our life, painless, blameless, peaceful, and a good defence before the dread judgement seat of Christ, let us ask of the Lord.

Choir: Grant this, O Lord.

At the conclusion of this litany the priest again says, 'Peace be with you,' and after the response 'And with thy spirit,' he says, 'Let us love one another that we may with one mind confess –' and the choir continues, 'The Father, Son, and Holy Ghost, Trinity consubstantial and undivided'. The Nicene Creed follows, after the deacon says, 'The doors, the doors, with wisdom let us attend.' The Creed may be sung by all, as it generally is in Russian churches, or it may be said by a single reader. During the Creed, the priest, with other priests if there are any present, lifts the aër and waves it over the Holy Gifts, kissing the cross in the middle of it at the words 'and ascended into heaven', folding it and putting it to one side.

The Holy Oblation now begins. The deacon says, 'Let us stand well; let us attend with fear. Let us attend, that we may offer the Holy Oblation in peace.' The choir then sings, 'A mercy of peace, a sacrifice of praise'. The priest says, 'The grace of our Lord Jesus Christ . . .' and then begins the Anaphora or Eucharistic Prayer, with the words 'Let us lift up our hearts'. The prayer, like the Latin Canon of the Mass, is addressed to God the Father. The part of the prayer until just before the Sanctus, the Latin Preface, is said secretly. It concludes (after a reference to the Cherubim and Seraphim which is not heard) with these words, usually said very loudly, 'singing, crying, shouting and saying the triumphal hymn', and the choir immediately sings, 'Holy, holy, holy . . .' The priest continues:

Priest: (*secretly*) We also, O merciful Master, with these celestial Powers cry and say, Holy art Thou and All-Holy, Thou and Thine only-begotten Son and Thy Holy Spirit. Holy art Thou and All-Holy and sublime is Thy Glory: Thou Who didst so love Thy world that Thou gavest Thine only-begotten Son, that whoso believeth on Him should not perish but have everlasting Life. And when He had come and fulfilled all that was needed for us, in the same night in which He was betrayed, or rather in which He gave Himself up for the life of the World, He took bread in His holy, pure and blameless Hands, and when He had given thanks and blessed and hallowed, He brake it and gave it to His Holy Disciples and Apostles, saying: (*aloud*) Take, eat: This is my Body which is broken for you, for the remission of sins.

Choir: Amen.

Priest: (*secretly*) Likewise after Supper the Cup, saying: (*aloud*) Drink ye all of It: This is My Blood of the New Testament, Which is shed for you and for many for the remission of sins.

Choir: Amen.

Priest: (*secretly*) Commemorating this command of our Saviour and all that He endured for our sake, the Cross, the Grave, the Resurrection after three days, the Ascension into Heaven, the Enthronement at the right hand of the Father, and the second and glorious Coming again, (*aloud*) Thine own of Thine own we offer to Thee, in all and for all.

Choir: We praise Thee, we bless Thee, we give thanks to Thee, O Lord, and we pray to Thee, O our God.

Priest: (*secretly*) Again we offer to Thee this reasonable and bloodless Service, and we ask and pray and supplicate: send down Thy Holy Spirit upon us and upon these Gifts here presented.

[*The Slavic Rite contains, in addition, these prayers, said as the Priest and Deacon bow three times before the Holy Table:*

Priest:	O Lord, Who didst send down Thy Most Holy Spirit at the third hour upon Thine Apostles: Take Him not from us, O Good One, but renew Him in us who pray unto Thee.
Deacon:	Create in me a clean heart, O God, and renew a right spirit within me.
Priest:	O Lord, Who didst send down Thy Most Holy Spirit . . .
Deacon:	Cast me not away from Thy presence, and take not Thy Holy Spirit from me.
Priest:	O Lord, Who didst send down Thy Most Holy Spirit . . .]
Deacon:	Master, consecrate the Holy Bread.
Priest:	And make this Bread the Precious Body of Thy Christ.
Deacon:	Amen. Master, consecrate the Holy Cup.
Priest:	And that which is in this Cup, the Precious Blood of Thy Christ.
Deacon:	Amen. Master, consecrate both Holy Things together.
Priest:	Changing (them) by Thy Holy Spirit.
Deacon:	Amen, Amen, Amen.

It is the whole of this prayer and not just the words of Christ that bring about the change of the Holy Gifts into the Body and Blood of Christ, completed by the words, 'changing them by Thy Holy Spirit'. The priest continues with a prayer that really follows straight on from this, beginning, 'that to them that shall partake thereof . . .' and the Thyateira translation, by the eminent scholar Archimandrite Ephrem Lash, does print it as a continuation with the rubric, 'the Priest, bowing profoundly, continues'. As this prayer is said the priest censes before the Holy Table and then the deacon censes round it, while the choir sings:

It is truly meet to bless thee, the Theotokos, ever-blessed and most-blameless, and Mother of our God. More honourable than the Cherubim, and beyond compare more glorious than the Seraphim, who without corruption gavest birth to God the Word, the very Theotokos, thee do we magnify.

As the priest's prayer continues, praying for the patriarch and the bishop, the deacon, at the Holy Door, exclaims, 'And those whom each one has in mind, and each and all', and the choir responds, 'and each and all', sometimes rendered as, 'and of all men and women'. There follows another 'again and again' litany prior to the Lord's Prayer, which is then introduced by the priest:

Priest: And vouchsafe, O Master, that with boldness and without condemnation we may dare to call upon Thee, the heavenly God and Father, and to say:

People: Our Father . . . but deliver us from the evil one.

Priest: For Thine is the Kingdom, and the power and the glory, of the Father, and of the Son, and of the Holy Spirit, now and ever, and unto the ages of ages.

Choir: Amen.

Priest: Peace be unto all.

Choir: And to thy spirit.

Deacon: Bow your head unto the Lord.

Choir: To Thee, O Lord.

The text alone inevitably conveys no sense of what happens when, after singing the Lord's Prayer, the whole congregation stands with bowed heads while the choir sings slowly, 'To Thee, O Lord,' and again a slow 'Amen' at the conclusion of the priest's prayer. The deacon, meanwhile, standing before the Holy Doors, changes his orarion so that it no longer hangs from his shoulder, but instead forms a cross. The deacon exclaims, 'Let us attend.' The Holy Doors are closed and the curtain drawn, to symbolize that Christ is in the tomb and the seal has been put on it. From within, elevating the Holy Bread, the priest says, 'The Holy Things for those who are Holy,' and the choir responds, 'One is Holy, One is Lord, Jesus Christ, in the glory of God the Father. Amen.'

The Lamb is now divided into four pieces and arranged on the paten like this:

IC

NI   KA

XC

The portion bearing the letters IC is placed in the chalice. The officiating clergy communicate from that marked XC, and the other two portions are used for the communion of the people. Some warm water is now poured into the chalice from a small ladle. It is known as the *zeon* and it symbolizes the gift of the Holy Spirit to the faithful in their communion. The clergy now make their communions in both kinds, first with the bread and then with the chalice.

Igumen Gregory Woolfenden's *Practical Handbook* explains what now happens behind the iconostasis:

> After this, the priest stands the holy chalice in its place on the antimension and reads the Prayer of Thanksgiving: *We thank Thee, O Master, Who lovest mankind . . .* and starts to divide the portions of the Lamb sealed with NI and KA. Reading the hymns: *We have seen the resurrection of Christ . . .*, he divides these portions into little particles, as many as necessary for all the communicants. Then the priest places all these particles into the chalice, covers the chalice with a small veil, and puts the spoon on top; the paten is covered with the star and the other small veil. After filling the chalice with the particles and having said the prayers appointed, the priest goes to the table of preparation, and takes a drink of blessed hot water and eats some antidoron (prosphora).

The curtain is drawn back, the Holy Doors are opened and the deacon and priest emerge, and those who wish to receive communion are invited to draw near. The faithful form a line coming from the south side of the temple, standing with hands crossed on their breasts, parents with young children going first. They whisper their Christian names, the communion cloth is spread beneath the mouth of the communicant and the priest gives communion in both kinds straight into the mouth by means of a spoon, saying, 'The servant of God (*name*) is made partaker of the pure and holy Body and Blood of the Lord and God and Saviour Jesus Christ, for the remission of sins and unto life everlasting.' The communicant's mouth is wiped with the cloth, and he or she kisses the chalice and then goes to the Table, towards the back of the temple on the north side, to receive the *zapivka* and the antidoron (at least in Russian churches). After all have received, the priest hands the chalice to the deacon, who places it on the Holy Table. The priest blesses the people with his hand, saying, 'O God, save your people, and bless your inheritance', and the choir sings:

> We have seen the true light; we have received the heavenly Spirit; we have found the true faith, as we worship the undivided Trinity; for the Trinity has saved us.

The particles on the paten are carefully wiped into the chalice and the priest censes it three times. The deacon takes the paten with the veil and asterisk and shows them to the people before taking them to the Prothesis. The priest, taking the chalice, says quietly, 'Blessed is our God,' and, showing the veiled chalice to the people, continues, 'Always, now and for ever, and unto the ages of ages'. The choir sings:

> Let our mouth be filled with Thy praise, O Lord, that we may extol Thy glory, for that Thou hast deigned to make us partakers of Thy holy, divine, immortal and life-giving mysteries. Establish us in Thy sanctification that all day long we may meditate upon Thy righteousness. Alleluia. Alleluia. Alleluia.

The priest places the chalice on the Prothesis, folds up the antimension and replaces the Gospel Book on the front of the Holy Table in the middle. The deacon, in his usual place, begins a short litany of thanksgiving, and the priest continues with a prayer of thanksgiving before the dismissal is said. There is a tendency in all liturgies for there to be a series of endings, and this is certainly true of the Orthodox Liturgy. The priest comes out through the Holy Doors and reads the Prayer Behind the Ambo, then goes back into the sanctuary and comes out again to bless the people. The concluding words vary in different versions.

Priest: The blessing of the Lord and His mercy be upon you, by His grace and love for mankind, always, now and for ever, and to the ages of ages.

Choir: Amen.

Priest: Glory to Thee, O God, our hope, glory to Thee.

Choir: Glory to the Father, and to the Son, and to the Holy Spirit; both now and for ever, and to ages of ages. Amen. Lord, have mercy (*three times*).
Holy Master, give the blessing.

Priest: May Christ, our true God (*on Sunday*: Who rose from the dead), have mercy upon us, through the intercession of His most pure and Holy Mother; through the virtue of the precious and life-giving Cross; through the protection of the precious Spiritual Powers in Heaven; through the supplications of the precious glorious Prophet and Forerunner John the Baptist; of the holy, glorious and honourable Apostles; of the holy, glorious and victorious Martyrs; of our saintly and holy Fathers; of the holy and righteous ancestors Joachim and Anna; of Saint (*of the day*), whose memory we celebrate, and of all the Saints, and may Christ save us through His goodness and compassion as our Merciful God.
Through the prayers of our holy Fathers have mercy upon us, O Lord Jesus Christ, our God.

Choir: Amen.

This concludes the Divine Liturgy, though the homily is often given here and the choir sings, 'Many years'. The priest offers the precious cross to the people to kiss and distributes the antidoron, then returns to the sanctuary, closes the Holy Doors and draws the curtain.

A note on translations

There is no common translation into English of the Liturgies of St Basil or St John Chrysostom or that of the Presanctified Gifts. The history of translation into English is itself quite an interesting one and some of the versions can be bought secondhand or be found in libraries. It begins, for scholarly and antiquarian purposes, with Covel in 1722 and King in 1772. There are erudite translations by the Victorian hymn-writer and Anglican divine John Mason Neale in the 1850s and 1860s. These were not intended for liturgical use, but to enable people to follow the service celebrated in Greek or Church Slavonic. The version by J. N. W. B. Robertson, published in 1886 with an expanded edition in 1894, which received patriarchal approval, contains an abundance of material from offices and liturgies in Greek–English parallel texts, with rubrics printed in red. In the preface to the 1886 version, Robertson says that the book is intended for the use of the Greek communities in London, Liverpool and Manchester, as well as for English-speaking travellers who attend the Greek Liturgy when abroad. He also says that the translation was undertaken at the request of Archimandrite Hieronymos Myriantheos. He was the priest of the Greek Church of St Saviour in Finsbury Circus in the City of London who laid the foundation stone for the new cathedral of St Sophia in Moscow Road, Bayswater, on 18 July 1877 and served the first Liturgy there on 1 June 1879. It is a pity the book lacks a table of contents and section headings, as this makes it almost unusable without a series of markers, which it also lacks.

A *Synopsis* in English, translated by a Lady Lechmere and published in 1890, was, it seems, from the letter of Nicodemus, the former Patriarch of Jerusalem, primarily intended to make Orthodox services better known to Anglicans. It has an excellent introduction, with a description of services, written by Joannes Gennadius (1844–1932), a Greek diplomat, scholar and bibliophile.

As ambassador in London, he had attended the laying of the foundation stone of St Sophia. Another volume that has endured, and is still available, is the *Service Book of the Holy Orthodox-Catholic Apostolic (Greco-Russian) Church* by Isabel F. Hapgood, an American Episcopalian (Anglican) who translated in rather wooden fashion some Russian literary classics and once stayed for a month with the Tolstoys. It was damned by the Roman Catholic liturgist Adrian Fortescue, who wrote, 'Not good; she knows neither theology nor liturgy, and her style is preposterous.' Not everyone shared Fortescue's view. The book, first published in America in 1906, appeared in a much improved second edition in 1922; there is, as Kallistos Ware wrote in 1963, a great deal of material to be found therein but, he added, 'the arrangement of this work is sometimes confusing and the translation not always satisfactory'. It was a translation from Slavonic and parts of it are still widely used. It is probably the first translation actually intended for liturgical use. Kuvochinsky's translation, also from the Slavonic, appeared in 1909 in a series of study editions of historic liturgical texts.

In 1914, there appeared a handy pocket or handbag edition of *The Divine Liturgy of St John Chrysostom* with Greek and English on opposite pages, which carried the note, 'The arrangement of this liturgy is that used in the Church of the Holy Wisdom in London.' A number of further volumes, in the same format and in purple covers, were published containing the Liturgy of the Presanctified, the services for Holy Week and Easter, for Epiphany and Pentecost, the sacraments of baptism, marriage and unction, and the service of Little Compline with the Akathist Hymn. The 1914 volume does not carry the name of the translator, but she can be identified as Alice Grace Elizabeth Carthew, born in 1867 into a wealthy family and a student at Girton College, Cambridge, from 1890. Her translation of the Divine Liturgy was published in a second edition by Faith Press in 1930. She died in London on 27 May 1940 and her funeral service was held, *The Times* announced, at the Greek Orthodox Cathedral, Moscow Road, W2.

Further texts and translations followed, mostly done by Anglicans. Notable were those of Herbert Hamilton Maughan in 1916, of Athelstan Riley (1858–1945), an adviser on Orthodox Churches to the Archbishop of Canterbury, and of the Oxford scholar F. E. Brightman in 1922. An influential translation from Slavonic was that of Patrick Thompson, published in 1939 for the Anglican–Orthodox Fellowship of St Alban and St Sergius. None of these were official, nor were they intended to be used for liturgical services. The last quarter of the twentieth century saw a number of official new translations including that of Archbishop Athenagoras of Thyateira and Great Britain in 1979, the Slavonic–English text of the Russian Orthodox Church Outside Russia in 1985 (generally known as the Jordanville text and now in its fourth edition, 2015), together with two from the learned Archimandrite Ephrem Lash for the Diocese of Thyateira in 1995 and 2011, an Australian Antiochian version in 1996 and a Sourozh text in 1999. Excellent translations of the *Lenten Triodion* and *Festal Menaion* were made in the 1970s by Mother Mary, of the Monastery of the Veil of the Mother of God, Bussy-en-Othe, and Metropolitan Kallistos Ware. Other texts, including the *Horologion* and *Menaion*, are also now available in American–English versions. As there is no single translation being used by all Orthodox churches in English-speaking countries there can be considerable textual differences.

Guidance on attending the Liturgy

Athelstan Riley's translation was part of a guide that he intended for travellers in Russia, Greece, Turkey and other countries with an Orthodox presence. He was uncertain whether there was demand for it and whether it was possible to present the Liturgy in a simple enough manner. It was only after the Great War that he produced his guide with the Liturgy in English and some common responses printed phonetically in Greek and in Slavonic 'to assist the English reader in regaining his track when he has temporarily lost himself'. Riley, an Anglican, acknowledged the help he received from Archdeacon Vladimir Theokritoff (1881–1950), who would be the priest of the Russian parish in London and in due course would have the young Anthony Bloom as his assistant. The guide contains some hints 'to aid the beginner in following a service which is so unfamiliar a type that it cannot help presenting considerable difficulties to him'. They are still useful and are given here in his own words (with editorial comments in square brackets). Riley assumed, in the manner of his age, that only men, and only Englishmen, would be venturing abroad!

1 There is only one liturgy in any church or chapel on the same day. At this, all the clergy attached to the church take part, the priests concelebrating, or assisting round the altar.

2 If there is no deacon his office is performed as far as possible by a priest but a priest never wears the deacon's vestments.

3 Avoid, if possible, a pontifical liturgy [that is, celebrated by a bishop, known in Orthodoxy as a hierarchical liturgy]. This is excessively complicated and the beginner will find a simple parochial liturgy with priest, deacon, and a reader quite complicated enough.

4 Try to be in time for the Liturgy and to note its commencement, remembering that there is usually a service somewhat analogous to [Anglican] Morning Prayer before it. The deacon coming out and standing before the Royal Doors and the commencement of the singing by the choir will give some sort of clue. At the end the liturgy often melts away into some other service, but this is not of such importance.

5 Watch the deacon carefully! You can hardly mistake the deacon. He wears an ungirded alb of coloured brocade and his stole hangs down straight, back and front, from his left shoulder. His normal place, when not inside the sanctuary with the priest, is in front of the Royal Doors. The priest remains, with few exceptions, in the sanctuary, and you do not see much of him.

6 Look out for the two Entrances [Lesser and Great]; you cannot mistake them, and they mark definite points in the service. [Riley also suggested watching the opening and closing of the Holy Doors, but there is no longer uniform practice with regard to this.]

7 Standing is the usual attitude of devotion in the East; if obliged to sit through weakness you will probably find a seat along the walls. As to kneeling, custom varies very much. The Russians usually kneel at the Great Entrance for the first part of the Cherubic Hymn, at the Sanctus till after the Consecration, and for the Lord's Prayer. But all this is a matter of private devotion. The self-conscious Englishman must try to realize that nobody is looking at him and nobody cares about what he does. Let him only behave quietly and reverently and all will be well. He need not kiss icons, or cross himself, or bow and prostrate himself unless he so desires, and he will be wise not to do these things unless they spring from a genuine devotion.

7

Music and musicians

The purpose of life, according to Gregory of Nyssa in his commentary on the psalms, *In inscriptiones Psalmorum*, is to make music, and true blessedness is to be found in the choir that unites human with angelic voices. It was in the music as much as in anything else that the Liturgy of the Great Church, as witnessed by Prince Vladimir's envoys, united earth and heaven. There is, of course, a history to liturgical music which shows that it departed from these celestial standards and, particularly in Russia, was influenced by developments in the West, as was the style of icon painting. It is a history that is as much concerned with the faith of composers as it is with musical styles. Kievan Rus' received from Constantinople all that was needed for the celebration of the Orthodox Liturgy: architecture, decoration, icons, texts and music. In every aspect the Greek and the Slavic gradually merged to produce a new form. In music this merger gave rise to chant notated in neumes and called, from the word *znamia*, meaning 'sign' or 'neume', *znamenny* (the same root as the title 'the Sign' given to the icon of the Theotokos). The types of chant identified by musicologist (and former bishop) Johann von Gardner are Znamenny or Stolp, Kievan, Greek, Bulgarian, Put' and Demestvenny Singing. There are some examples of a form of polyphony, a kind of descant style, with the chant harmonized by two voices, one above and one below, known as *troyestrochnoye*, 'three-line singing'. During the ill-fated liturgical reforms of Patriarch Nikon, formerly of Novgorod, an hierodeacon came from Constantinople to teach Greek chant, which he did in 1656–1659. The so-called Greek chant written down in Russian musical manuscripts has nothing in common with genuine Byzantine chant; to quote one musical scholar, 'its highly individual intervals and intonation was poles apart from that practised in the Greek Church'. It was a genuinely Slavonic form and lighter and simpler than *znamenny*; its use tended to shorten services.

It was not until the eighteenth century that Russian enthusiasm for Italian music, and especially opera, seriously influenced liturgical singing. The musicians were Roman Catholics. The Empress Elizabeth (1741–1762) created a small Italian-style Imperial Cappella. Catherine the Great (1762–1796) appointed the Italian composer Baldassare Galuppi, a Venetian pupil of Antonio Lotti, as Director of the Court Theatre and *maestro di capella*, 1765–1768. Some fourteen of his church works are extant and demonstrate an effective blending of Italian rococo harmonies and Slavonic texts. He was followed by Giovanni Paisiello and Giuseppe Sarti. In 1772 the Holy Synod (the governing body of the Russian Church after Peter the Great abolished the Moscow Patriarchate) published a collection of traditional chants for the most common services in conscious opposition to the dominance of foreign styles. The Ukrainian-born Dimitry Bortnyansky (1751–1825) was a chorister of the Imperial Chapel, to which he returned in 1779, after eleven years of study in Italy. He defined the style of liturgical music for more than half a century and his compositions were praised by Berlioz, Tchaikovsky (who edited a ten-volume edition of his choral works) and Rimsky-Korsakov. He also secured a musical monopoly for the Director of the Imperial Chapel. New compositions had no connection with the old chants which were, however, preserved in provincial monasteries, villages and poor towns that could not afford a trained choir to sing in the fashionable Italian style. However, Bortnyansky, who had to follow the popular style and fashion in his compositions, studied and harmonized traditional chants in his spare time and was behind the 1810 'Project on printing ancient Russian neumatic singing'. The 'sacred concertos', which now became popular, were pieces sung during the priest's communion, when the Holy Doors were closed with the curtain drawn; they were not considered strictly a part of the Liturgy and so could be more Italianate. They were developed in a magisterial way by another, and younger, Ukrainian who also studied in Italy,

Maxim Berezovsky (1745–1777), *maestro di capella* from 1774 until his premature death, and combined classical-style choral work with the tradition of *a capella* singing. Noëlle Mann, editor of the Oxford volume *Russian Sacred Music for Choirs*, points to the significance of one of his three remaining concertos, out of eighteen known to us. It is a setting of Psalm 71.9–13, 'Do not reject me in my old age', and in her words, 'the tragic emotional intensity of this masterpiece ensured its role in the development of Russian music, both sacred and secular'.

P. I. Tchaikovsky shared with a great many educated Russians of his day an attitude to the Church characterized by three things: a broad acceptance of Christian ethics, a regretful rejection of Christian doctrines and an artistic, or sentimental, pleasure in church ritual. In 1877 he wrote that his reason 'obstinately refuses to recognise as true the dogmatic aspects of Orthodoxy', whereas, as a consequence of his education and the habits of his childhood, he still turned to Christ 'with prayers in sorrow and with gratefulness in happiness'. Yet when Madame von Meck wrote, in November 1877, that she had no religion 'as it is generally understood' and only went to church every two years, to confession and communion, 'as an example to the servants', Tchaikovsky replied that his attitude to the Church was quite different:

For me it has retained much of its poetic charm. I very often go to the Eucharist; the Liturgy of St John Chrysostom, in my opinion, is one of the greatest of all artistic creations. If you follow the service carefully and try to grasp the meaning of every ritual, it is impossible not to be moved in spirit when present at one of our Orthodox services. I am also fond of the Vigil Service. To go to some ancient, small church on Saturday, stand in semi-darkness, the air thick with the smoke of incense, to withdraw into oneself, and ponder the eternal questions: *what for? when? whither? why?*, and then to be drawn out of oneself again by the choir singing: '*From my youth up many passions afflict me*' and surrender oneself to the fascinating poetry of the psalm, to be filled with quiet delight when the Royal Doors are flung open and '*Praise the Lord from the heavens!*' rings out – oh, I love it all awfully, it is one of my supreme pleasures!

But after this hymn of praise, and affirming that he was still bound to the Church by very strong ties, he declared, 'like you, I lost all faith in doctrines long ago'. At the end of the following April he writes:

if my present good frame of mind lasts, I'd like to do something for church music. This is a huge and almost virgin territory for the composer. I recognise that Bortnyansky, Berezovsky, and co., have some value, but their music doesn't harmonise well with Byzantine-architecture, ikons, and the whole ethos of Orthodox worship. Did you know that composing for the Church is the monopoly of the Imperial Chapel, and that it is forbidden to print, or to sing in church, anything not published by the Chapel, who guard this monopoly zealously and do not want any new settings of sacred texts to be attempted? . . . I may well decide to set the whole liturgy of St John Chrysostom.

He did, and his publisher, Jurgenson, found a way to publish it in 1878. In 1880 they got a judicial ruling that effectively abolished the Chapel's monopoly and opened the way for more liturgical compositions. Much new Orthodox music was composed from then until the Revolution of 1917.

After setting the Liturgy, Tchaikovsky went on to set a number of the hymns from the All-Night Vigil. Before doing this he studied the texts and asked the advice of various priests, who were not much help to him, about what was needed. When one priest friend admitted that his sexton arranged all the services, he said, 'If even priests don't know, how am I, a poor sinner, to resolve it?' He received help from the first professor of the history and theory of church music at the Moscow Conservatoire, Dmitry Razumovsky, who was appointed in 1866. He completed the *Vigil* in 1881 and, after an audience with Alexander III in 1884, at his suggestion he composed *Nine Sacred Pieces* drawn from a number of different services, published the next year. Between writing the *Liturgy* and the *Sacred Pieces*, Tchaikovsky had returned to the Orthodox faith. In 1879 he found himself deeply moved by reading Dostoevsky's *The Brothers Karamazov* and shaken, 'moved into sobbing and hysteria', by the scene in which Elder Zosima receives the sick. By 1884 he considered himself an Orthodox believer and he wrote, 'Every day, every hour, I thank God for having given me this faith in him.' In 1886 he went into Moscow's Uspensky Cathedral and found that his setting of the *Liturgy* was being performed, and he was overjoyed as his music and his faith had come together.

Two musical schools developed in the next few years. The German or St Petersburg School (Arkhangelsky, Lvovsky, Lvov, Rimsky-Korsakov, Balakirev, Tchaikovsky) did not insist on using traditional chants as the sole criterion of spirituality, unlike the Moscow School, and freely applied the principles of Western polyphony to their work. Their compositions do not therefore sound as unmistakably Russian as those of the Moscow School (Kastalsky, Smolensky, Taneyev, Chesnokov, Grechaninov, Rachmaninov). A leading influence in Moscow was Stepan Smolensky (1848–1909), described by Kastalsky as 'an indefatigable toiler in the archaeological field of church music', who had studied chant since the early 1870s and succeeded Razumovsky at the Conservatoire. Among the most influential composers was Pavel Chesnokov (1877–1944) who went to the Moscow Conservatoire as a student in 1913 at the age of thirty-six, when he was already an established composer and choir director, having studied composition with Smolensky at the Synodal School. He followed Kastalsky and Grechaninov in their respect for traditional chants. By 1917 he was acknowledged as a giant of Russian sacred music. He remained in Russia after the Revolution and was choir director of the Cathedral of Christ the Saviour in Moscow until its demolition by the Soviets in 1931.

When we turn to Russian composers renowned for their secular music, we find, perhaps surprisingly, that there are twenty-two sacred compositions by Nikolai Rimsky-Korsakov. The best-known of these is the 'Our Father' from his setting of the Liturgy of

John Chrysostom, Op. 22. Concerning his *Russian Easter Festival Overture*, which some said captured the legendary and heathen side of the feast in preference to its Christian elements, he wrote a passage that shows he expects few educated people to have any acquaintance with Orthodox services:

> In any event, in order to appreciate my Overture even ever so slightly, it is necessary that the hearer should have attended Easter morning service at least once, and that not in a domestic chapel, but in a cathedral thronged with people from every walk of life with several priests conducting the cathedral service – something that many intellectual Russians, let alone hearers of other confessions, quite lack nowadays. As for myself, I have gained impressions, in my childhood, passed near the Tikhvin Monastery itself [120 miles east of St Petersburg].

It is often said of another noted composer of secular and religious music, Sergei Rachmaninov (1873–1943), that he was not religious; it would be truer to say that he kept his religious views to himself. His setting of the Liturgy of St John Chrysostom (1910) carries the epigraph 'Thanks be to God', suggesting that he may have come to share Tchaikovsky's outlook, if not his faith. Whereas his Liturgy uses his own thematic material, the so-called *Vespers* Op. 37 (really a setting of hymns from the *All-Night Vigil, Vsenoshchnoye bdeniye*), written for the Synodal Choir in 1915, uses old monophonic Greek and Russian chants from the Synod's collections. Rachmaninov had strong memories of church services in the monasteries and cathedrals of Novgorod, where he was taken by his grandmother, and these influenced this work, which was dedicated to the memory of Stepan Smolensky. It had only been given concert performances before the prohibition of public performances of sacred music introduced by the Bolsheviks in 1917. It was first sung during a service in Moscow in 1957 in memory of the composer, and annually thereafter. The development of Orthodox church music continued in the post-revolution emigration, especially in Paris, with composers continuing the traditions of the Moscow School; there are several excellent recordings of their compositions. At a conference in 2008, Patriarch Kirill of Moscow observed that, in the diaspora, Russian sacred music was not only preserved but also developed and revealed to the non-Orthodox. The choir of the St Sergius Theological Academy in Paris regularly sang fundraising concerts in Britain between the wars and introduced many people to Orthodox music.

Two modern composers are known for being Orthodox, John Tavener (1944–2013) and Arvo Pärt (b. 1935). For a period the former set clearly Orthodox texts, though his settings would have mostly been unsuitable for liturgical use. The other, with a very occasional exception, has not set liturgical texts and yet his music seems in other ways to express Orthodox spirituality.

Tavener always said that he entered the Russian door of Orthodoxy, being prepared and received by Metropolitan Anthony Bloom, though the Greek side of his life and character was really dominant and Metropolitan Kallistos Ware officiated at his funeral, an Orthodox service in an Anglican cathedral. His first work after becoming Orthodox, *Palintropos* (1977), written on the island of Patmos, was, he said, related to Orthodoxy by way of the Orthodox belief that man and nature are basically divine on account of the Incarnation. He worked with Orthodox theologian Sergei Haeckel on the *Akhmatova Requiem* (1979) and produced a setting of part of the *Great Canon of St Andrew of Crete* (1981) and a setting of the *All-Night Vigil* (1984). Much influenced by the Orthodox nun Mother Thekla, he said that he wanted to make icons in sound. After a period of fruitful spiritual and artistic cooperation, which included his second opera *Mary of Egypt* (1992) and the 'Song for Athene' (1993), they reportedly parted company in 2003 as Tavener became more universalist in his views and in his music, and much of his music became massive. The most accessible music from what has been called his Orthodox period (1980s–1990s) includes *Ikon of Light* (especially the two settings of the Trisagion), the superb *Funeral Ikos* and the *Great Canon*.

Arvo Pärt grew up in a Lutheran family in Soviet Estonia and also became Orthodox in the 1970s. The 'Orthodoxy' of his music is much less about setting liturgical texts – and indeed most of what he has set is from the Latin liturgy – and more about express-ing the simplicity, purity and silence that belong to the Orthodox ascetical and mystical tradition as an antidote to a prevailing cul-ture that is complex, sullied and noisy. The Orthodox theologian Peter Bouteneff, who knows Pärt well and has written a book about him, says that he is a deeply ecumenical person, the antithesis of an Orthodox zealot or exclusivist, but – and this is what is truly important – Orthodoxy is where he resides spiritually. The same qualities can be found in his music, whether choral or purely in-strumental, as in the Church's liturgy, where music constitutes an indispensable part of the experience, not least in facilitating the communication of the text, perhaps through repeated musical phrases, perhaps through direct musical expression. The settings of texts with a distinctly Orthodox flavour include his *Bogoroditse Djevo* and *Triodion* (a setting of three odes, sung in English) and three perhaps unexpectedly wonderful pieces: *The Beatitudes*, *The Woman with the Alabaster Jar* and a really amazing setting of the genealogy from Luke's Gospel, inspired by the transmission of names in Iceland, *Which was the Son of . . .* A third Orthodox composer, worthy of note but less well known and deserving to be better known, is the theologian, musicologist and priest, Ivan Moody. His compositions reflect his research interests embracing twentieth-century and contemporary music in the pan-Ortho-dox world and its relations not only to spirituality and theology but to the aesthetics of modernism and post-modernism. Of par-ticular note are his *Canticum Canticorum I–IV*, his setting of the *Troparian of Kassiani, Apokathilosis* (recorded by Nigel Short and Tenebrae), 'The Akathistos Hymn' (recorded by another distin-guished Orthodox musicologist Alexander Lingas with Cappella Romana) and especially his *Passion and Resurrection* (recorded by Cappella Amsterdam).

A choice of recordings

Rimsky-Korsakov is right to define as two separate experiences Orthodox services in a small church or domestic chapel and in a

great cathedral or monastery. Some of the finest Russian liturgical music can be appreciated in concert performance, but this is
still quite different from liturgical performance, where the setting
combines with the ritual action and the music. The full liturgical
experience with large musical resources can really only be found
in Russian and Eastern European cathedrals and monasteries with
strong musical traditions, such as those found in Ukraine and
Bulgaria. There is always a risk in suggesting favourites, but the
following would provide an adequate cross-section of Orthodox
music.

Though Byzantine chant is something of an acquired taste,
the excellent multivolume series 'Byzantine Music of the Greek
Orthodox Church' offers a great variety with a high standard of
performance and recording. To be recommended as an introduction are the 'Doxology' (vol. 1) and the 'Thrice-Holy Hymn' (vol. 10).

For medieval Russian chant, there is a recording by that remark-
able bishop, musician and scholar, Metropolitan Hilarion Alfeyev
with the Danilov monastery choir in *The Divine Liturgy of St John
Chrysostom: Medieval chant of the Russian Orthodox Church*.

A marvellous recording from a mixed Bulgarian choir is entitled *Good Friday: Bulgarian Orthodox Liturgy*. Four tracks are
exceptionally beautiful examples of Orthodox music with the titles
'Grave-Wailing (Lamentations)', 'Eulogitarium', 'Great Doxology'
and the 'Mournful Holy God' (being a mournful setting of the
Trisagion).

For both chant and later compositions, there is an album from
Ukraine entitled *Selected Chants of the Russian Orthodox Church*
by the Monks' Choir of the Kiev Pechersky monastery, though the
mixed Kiev Metropolitan Choir also sings on the recording. In an
overall excellent recording, three tracks require high commenda-
tion: 'Thy Resurrection, O Christ', which is authentic Kiev chant
from the Easter Vigil, 'O God Forgive Me' and the 'Great Doxology'.

Composers of late nineteenth-century and pre-Revolutionary
Russia are well represented in recordings. Four, by very different ensembles, should receive special recommendation. They
are Chesnokov's *Liturgy* Op. 42, engagingly recorded by the

Moscow Church of the Most Holy Mother of God Birth Choir, Arkhangelsky's *All-Night Vigil* by the Cantus Sacred Music Ensemble, Grechaninov's *Passion Week* Op. 58, perhaps surprisingly by the Phoenix Bach Chorale, and, in the Series 'Chants of the Russian Empire', Ledkovsky's sacred music performed by the Resurrection Church Choir of Moscow.

There are many recordings of all or parts of the Liturgy of St John Chrysostom set by Tchaikovsky. As the superb recording by the State Capella Choir of St Petersburg is no longer available, the best alternative seems to be that of the National Choir of the Ukraine, 'Dumka'. Rachmaninov's sublime setting of the *Hymns of the All-Night Vigil* is best recorded on an imported CD by the Choir of St Nicholas Church in Tolmachi at the State Tretyakov Gallery or, if that is not available, in the album incorrectly entitled *Vespers* from the MDR Rundfunkchor Leipzig.

Ivan Moody, who both studied theology at Joensuu in Eastern Finland and was Professor of Church Music there, has a rare appreciation of the particular richness of Finnish Orthodoxy. He explores this musically in the album *Arctic Light: Finnish Orthodox Music*, in which he directs Cappella Romana.

Finally, there is the liturgical singing in English, though with American voices. St Vladimir's Seminary Choir, in New York State, has issued a number of recordings. One, *Vigil – Selections from the All-Night Vigil*, has a really interesting example of an English text of the Great Doxology sung to Russian chant.

If it was a choice of just one track from one album to express the beauty of Russian Orthodox church music, the choice would fall on Arkhangelsky's setting of the Great Doxology, though certainly in competition with settings of the same text by Rachmaninov, Grechaninov, Ippolitov-Ivanov and Kastalsky. The Great Doxology is the Orthodox version of the Latin 'Gloria in excelsis', from which it differs in a number of ways, incorporating verses from the psalms (Psalms 35.10 (36.9), 89 (90).1 and 118 (119).12) and concluding with the Trisagion. To appreciate a recording fully it is generally helpful to have a transliteration of the Church Slavonic, which is given here with a literal English translation.

Slavoslovie velikoe

Slava v vyshnikh Bogu, i na zemli mir, v chelovetsekh blagovole-
nie. Khvalim Tya, blagoslovim Tya, klanyaem Ti sya, slavoslovim
Tya, blagodarim Tya, velikiya radi slavy Tvoeya. Gospodi
Tsaryu Nebesnyi, Bozhe Otche Vsederzhitelyu, Gospodi, Syne
Edinorodnyi, Iisuse Khriste, i Svyatyi Dushe. Gospodi Bozhe,
Agnche Bozhii, Syne Otech', vzemlyai grekh mira, pomilui nas;
vzemlyai grekhi mira, priimi molitvu nashu; sedyai odesnuyu
Ottsa, pomilui nas. Yako Ty esi edin Svyat, Ty esi edin Gospod',
Iisus Khristos, v slavu Bogu Ottsa, amin'.

Na vsyak den' blagoslovlyu Tya, i voskhvalyu imya Tvoe vo veki,
i v vek veka.

Spodobi, Gospodi, v den' sei bez grekha sokhranitisya nam.
Blagosloven esi, Gospodi, Bozhe otets nashikh, i khval'no i proslav-
leno imya Tvoe vo veki, amin'.

Budi, Gospodi, milost' Tvoya na nas, yakozhe upovakhom na
Tya.

Blagosloven esi, Gospodi, nauchi mya opravdaniem Tvoim
(trizhdy).

Gospodi, pribezhishche byl esi nam v rod i rod. Az rekh:
Gospodi, pomilui mya, istseli dushu moyu, yako sogreshikh Tebe.

Gospodi, k Tebe pribegokh, nauchi mya tvoriti volyu Tvoyu,
yako Ty esi Bog moi: yako u Tebe istochnik zhivota, vo svete Tvoem
uzrim svet. Probavi milost' Tvoyu vedushchim Tya.

Svyatyi Bozhe, Svyatyi Krepkii, Svyatyi Bezsmertnyi, pomilui
nas *(trizhdy).*

Slava Ottsa i Syna i Svyatago Dukha, nyne i prisno i vo veki ve-
kov. Amin'.

Svyatyi Bezsmertnyi, pomilui nas.

Svyatyi Bozhe, Svyatyi Krepkii, Svyatyi Bezsmertnyi, pomilui
nas.

Glory to God in the highest

Glory to God in the highest, and on earth
peace, goodwill towards men.
We praise Thee; we bless Thee; we worship

Thee, we give thanks to Thee for Thy great glory.

O Lord, Heavenly King, God the Father Almighty.

O Lord the Only-begotten Son, Jesus Christ, and the Holy Spirit.

O Lord God, Lamb of God, Son of the Father, that takest away the sins of the world: have mercy on us; Thou that takest away the sins of the world, hear our prayer. Thou that sittest at the right hand of the Father, have mercy upon us.

For Thou only art holy, Thou only art the Lord, Jesus Christ, to the glory of God the Father. Amen.

Every day I will bless Thee, O Lord; keep us this day without sin.

Thou art blessed, O Lord, God of our fathers, and praised and worshipped be Thy Name to the ages. Amen.

Let, O Lord, Thy kindness be on us, for we trust in Thee.

Thou art blessed, O Lord, teach me Thy statutes (*three times*).

O Lord, Thou hast been our refuge from one generation to another.

I said: O Lord, have mercy on me, heal my soul, for I have sinned against Thee.

O Lord, I run to Thee, teach me to do Thy will, for Thou art my God:

for in Thee, O Lord, is the source of life, and in Thy light shall we see light.

Extend Thy kindness to those who trust in Thee.

Holy God, Holy Mighty, Holy Immortal,
   have mercy upon us (*three times*).
Glory to the Father and to the Son and to
   the Holy Ghost, now and for ever,
   and unto the ages of ages. Amen.
Holy Immortal, have mercy upon us.
Holy God, Holy Mighty, Holy Immortal,
   have mercy upon us.

8

Orthodoxy and literature

As we can see from the relationship between liturgy and music, Orthodoxy is a culture as well as a religion. As such, it has clearly left an impression on Russian literature. The writer Anton Chekhov (1860–1904) attended the Greek school in the town of his birth, Taganrog on the Sea of Azov, from 1867 to 1879, and there received an Orthodox religious education. He and his brothers sang in the church choir, which was conducted by their father; they read the epistles and psalms in church and served as altar boys and bell-ringers. Apparently, Chekhov looked back on the experience as rather gloomy and later lost his faith, but, as Richard Pevear says in the introduction to Chekhov's *Stories*, his familiarity with church life shows in many of them and his knowledge of the services and prayers was probably more precise than that of any other writer. Once you know something about Orthodox beliefs, services and vestments, it is more fun to read Chekhov's stories about bishops, priests, monks and the devout Russian laity. Not only can one say, with some satisfaction, 'I know what he's talking about' when he tells of Father Grigory 'standing by the north door, still in his vestments' or of Bishop Pyotr standing 'motionless in the middle of the church through all twelve Gospel readings' and finding that 'his legs had gone quite numb, so that he gradually ceased to feel them', but one can learn more about what Fedotov called the Russian religious mind, which is still such a feature of Slavic Orthodoxy. In Chekhov we find fasting and feasting, the dull days of Great Lent and the bright days of Easter Week, the lists of names for commemoration, on separate sheets for the living and the dead, sent to the sanctuary with some prosphoras, the small round loaves used for the Eucharist, the *kulich* for the living and the *kolivo*, or *kutya*, for the dead, *akathists* and *panikhidas*, the sick Marfa being given communion at home and being anointed with oil, the pussy-willow on Palm Sunday and green branches and flowers at Pentecost, together with quotations from hymns, prayers and readings.

Particularly worth reading is 'Panikhida', which takes place completely in a church staffed by priest, deacon, beadle and caretaker. Despite the slanting ray of sunlight passing through the bluish smoke streaming from the censer, Chekhov finds the church empty, lifeless and gloomy. 'Easter Night' tells of the cannon shots and burning tar barrels that marked the night of the Resurrection of Christ and the whole crowd around a monastery full of general joyful excitement. The Twelve Gospels are central to the story entitled 'The Student', as they are to 'The Bishop', which is set in Great and Holy Week. Orthodox faith and everyday life are inextricably linked in the story 'In the Ravine'.

Leo Tolstoy (1828–1910) had an ambivalent relationship with the Orthodox Church and was excommunicated by the Russian Holy Synod in 1901. His stories often involve criticism of the Church, icons, monasteries, elders, pilgrims and so on, while demonstrating his deep knowledge of hagiography and ecclesiastical practice. His stories 'Father Sergius' and 'The Forged Coupon' were both published posthumously. 'Father Sergius' tells of a Russian prince and officer who joins a monastery after being told by his fiancée that she has been the Tsar's mistress. He becomes a monk for all the wrong reasons, embraces monastic discipline eventually becoming a recluse, discovers the power of healing and attracts many pilgrims. Still attractive to and attracted by women, he resists the seduction of one noblewoman only by cutting off his finger, but is seduced by a sick girl who comes to him for help. After this, he flees the monastery and ends up being sent to Siberia as a vagabond. A detailed analysis would bring out the relationship of this story to the stories of the Desert Fathers and to the sort of narrative found in the paterika, including the accounts that tell of the moral failings to which recluses were prone. Tolstoy is well acquainted with and critical of the tradition of the monastic elders. Sergius's abbot had a distinguished spiritual genealogy, from St Paisius Velichovsky to Elder

Amvrosy of Optina. It might be Tolstoy's point that none of this brought any benefit to the monk Sergius, though it has been suggested that the monk's life parallels that of the author himself in his latter years, when he enjoyed a fame of which he considered he was not worthy. Whatever the case, 'Father Sergius' is strongly influenced by monastic life in the Russian Orthodox Church. 'The Forged Coupon' includes the story of an encounter between a group of sectarians, gospel-evangelicals who have stopped going to church and taken down their icons, with a rather stuffy Archimandrite, Father Misail, who asks whether it is true that they called the holy icons 'boards'. A peasant named Ivan Chuyev, who tries to do everything according to God's law, replies, 'Well, you just turn any old icon round and see for yourself.'

Many people know about Orthodoxy from Dostoevsky's *The Brothers Karamazov* (1880) and we saw what an impact it had on Tchaikovsky. Some say that in the communist period in Russia, most knowledge of religion was conveyed through literature such as this. Dostoevsky's staretz Elder Zosima is now investigated as if he were a true source of spiritual knowledge, a saint like Sergius of Radonezh or Seraphim of Sarov. This is simply not the case and it would be wise to heed the warning of Dmitry Petrovich Svyatopolk-Mirsky (D. S. Mirsky), who taught English and Russian Literature at the University of London from 1921 until he returned to Russia in 1932. Arrested in 1937, he died in the gulag in 1939. He wrote:

But the truth is (and here lies the exceptional significance of Dostoevsky as a spiritual case) that the tragedies of Dostoevsky are irreducible tragedies that cannot be solved or pacified. His harmonies and his solutions are all on a lower or shallower level than his conflicts and his tragedies. To understand Dostoevsky is to accept his tragedies as irreducible and not to try to shirk them by the contrivances of his smaller self. His Christianity in particular is of a very doubtful kind. It is impossible to overlook the fact that it was no ultimate solution to him, that it did not reach into the ultimate depths of his soul, that it was a more or less superficial spiritual formation which it is dangerous to identify with real Christianity.

'Different days of the Church Year produce in us different spiritual feelings', writes Father Sergei Bulgakov. 'The air we breathe on weekdays appears to differ from what we breathe on Sundays; and both differ from great feasts. And completely exceptional in our life is the period of the Great Fast.' We see this in Russian novels, short stories and memoirs. The writer Teffi (pseudonym of Nadezhda Alexandrovna Lokhvitskaya, 1872–1952) describes Holy Saturday, when she was a young girl, as 'a solemn, anxious day'. There were no lessons and children were not allowed to play; her elder sisters were sitting in the dining room, decorating eggs. There was the question of whether she would be taken to the Easter Vigil. She remembered Easter morning as always bright and cheerful and how, going to the dining room where the adults were drinking tea and breaking the fast after the Liturgy, she would come back with 'half a hard-boiled egg, a piece of *kulich* and a piece of *pashka*'. She describes the church, on what must again be Great and Holy Thursday night with the Twelve Gospels, as crowded and stuffy.

Candles splutter quietly in the hands of the worshippers. A pale blue blanket of incense smoke spreads out high in the dome. Down below – the gold of the icons, black figures and the flames of candles. All around – black, candlelight and gold.

She remembers Holy Thursday again on board the ship crowded with those fleeing from the Bolsheviks when, across the waters from a town still held by the Whites, she hears the bells booming out, and observes that this is a sound she has known all her life, one that takes hold of her soul and leads it past the screams and bloodshed of the Revolution to the simple, sweet days of her childhood.

It was in 1921 that the sixteen-year-old Lesley Blanch was taken to the Easter Night service in Paris by a Russian friend of her parents, referred to only as 'the Traveller'. In her autobiographical fragments, *Journey into the Mind's Eye*, she tells of them making their way by taxi to the rue Daru and being forced to a standstill at the corner of the rue de la Néva by the large crowds converging on the Russian Cathedral. On foot, they edged through the hushed, exalted throng.

Within the church, all is dark, anguished, still, as priests and people alike await the moment when Christ is risen.

She was surprised, having got in, to be propelled out again as the Traveller decided to wait for the procession outside and explained how the circling of the church expressed the hesitation, the doubts of the disciples, finding Christ vanished from the sepulchre. Thus, he says, the procession goes to search for Christ outside the walls and, the third time, accepts the miracle, entering again to proclaim the Resurrection.

As we waited, the night air smelled damp and fresh, the scent of the early lilac in the courtyard overcoming the wafts of incense that floated from the church along with snatches of muffled chanting. At their windows the French householders stood silent, sharing something of the tension. Just before midnight the church doors swung open and in a flood of colour and candlelight the glittering procession emerged to circle the building three times, chanting. The long tapers they carried sparkled on the sumptuous brocaded vestments and the diamond-studded crowns of the Metropolitan and high clergy. Gold-coped priests and acolytes swung censers and carried banners and ikons, all glowing out from the darkness. At last, with measured tread, grave in their joy, they re-entered the church, there to announce to the waiting throng that Christ was Risen. We heard a sudden burst of singing, rapturous music, and the bells rang out overhead.

Christos Vosskress! Christ is Risen. Yea, verily He is Risen!

The crowds joined in the great cry, crossing themselves, prostrating themselves, kissing each other, friends and strangers, each saluted with the triple kisses of the Trinity.

It is not just the externals of Orthodoxy that appear in memoirs and literature. Theology, as found in liturgical texts, can also seem to appear in unlikely places. St Petersburg intellectual Boris Nikolai Bugaev (1880–1934) wrote under the pseudonym Andrei Bely. His novel *Petersburg* (1916) has been said to do for the Russian language what *Ulysses* did for English. There is a curious scene in which the central character, Nikolai Apollonovich Ableukhov, has a dream in which all bodies cease to be bodies:

> Bereft of body, still he felt his body: some invisible centre that had previously been both his consciousness and his 'self', turned out to possess a semblance of the former burned to ashes: Nikolai Apollonovich's logical premises turned into bones; the syllogisms around these bones wrapped themselves into rigid sinews; the content of his logical activity developed flesh and skin; and so the 'self' of Nikolai Apollonovich again displayed its bodily form, although it was not a body; and in this *non-body* (in the exploded 'self') someone else's 'self' was revealed: this 'self' had rushed in from Saturn and to Saturn it returned.

In the next moment he is seated, in the dream, before his father, in just the same way that he used to sit before, but now without a body – 'without a body, but in a body (a strange business!)' – which seems to mimic the 'strange' references found in the liturgy and identified in Chapter 1.

Inevitably, given they were to be found in homes as well as churches, icons feature in many stories. There is not much religion in the celebrated novel *A Hero of Our Time* by Mikhail Lermontov (1814–1841). The people at the spa never go to church and are far more interested in fate and destiny than they are in divine providence, but Grigory Alexandrovich Pechorin, the Byronic hero of the book, goes into the house of a suspected criminal and we realize that 'there wasn't a single icon on the walls – a bad sign!' In Bely's *Petersburg* Alexandr Ivanonich Dudkin, despite being a revolutionary, wears a silver cross beneath his shirt and has a small icon over his bed, depicting the thousand nights of prayer by Seraphim of Sarov, on a rock amid the pine trees.

We have already seen, when dealing with clerical dress and vestments, that Nikolai Semyonovich Leskov (1831–1895) used to great effect his memories of visiting Russian monasteries with his grandmother in his book *The Cathedral Clergy*. He must have heard many of the sort of stories found in the paterika and clearly this one, concerning a cavalry officer and an elderly bishop and involving prayer, icons and fasting, was among his favourites:

'This fine gentleman,' Tuganov went on, 'learned that no one had ever dined with your bishop, and he made a wager at the club with the chief of police that he would dine with him, but as ill luck would have it, the old man found out about it! . . .'

'Oh, no! Oh, no-o-o!' Zacharias exclaimed.

'Well, sir, this cavalry officer went to visit him and he sat there and sat there until the bishop got back from mass [the Liturgy], and then he sat there some more. Finally he couldn't stand it any longer and when it was past six he got up to leave. But the silent bishop, who until then had only listened to him without speaking, said, "Say, why don't you stay and eat with me!" Well, his guest immediately pricked up his ears – he'd won the wager. The bishop kept him waiting there another hour and then led the way to the table.'

'Oh, he shouldn't have done that,' said Zacharias. 'No, he shouldn't.'

'Please allow me to continue. When they entered the dining room, the bishop went and stood in front of an icon and started to pray, and he prayed, and he prayed, one prayer after another. And another hour went by; his famished guest could scarcely stay on his feet. "All right, you may serve dinner now," the reverend bishop finally said. They were given two tiny bowls of pea soup with crackers, and just when the officer's appetite had been whetted, the reverend bishop stood up again. "Now let us give thanks," he said, "unto the Lord God for our repast." But this time, when he began to pray, our brave lad didn't wait around – he tiptoed out and fled. The old man told me this story yesterday and laughed. "That spirit," he said, "could in nowise be cast out save through prayer and fasting."'

Dr Zhivago, the epic novel by Boris Pasternak (1890–1960), in print and in film, introduced many people to Russia and the Revolution. Although it may be said to carry a powerful theme of resurrection it is, like Lara, not explicitly religious.

> Lara was not religious. She did not believe in rites. But sometimes, in order to endure life, she needed it to be accompanied by some inner music. She could not invent such music each time for herself. This music was the word of God about life, and Lara went to church to weep over it.

Yuri Zhivago, and perhaps Pasternak himself, carried the sort of residual Orthodoxy already seen in Tchaikovsky and Rimsky-Korsakov. Zhivago's memories are associated with his mother and with her death:

> It was as if it dipped into the gilded basin in their nursery and, having bathed in fire and gold, turned into an early or late liturgy in the little church in the lane where his nanny took him. There the stars of the sky became icon lamps, dear God became the priest, and everyone was assigned his duties more or less according to ability.

We find Orthodoxy also in some Russian poetry, starting from the *dukhóvnye stikhí*, the oft-recited oral religious poems, literally spiritual verses, composed anonymously between the fifteenth and seventeenth centuries; an example is 'The Saturday of St Dimitri' (the Saturday before his feast still being one of the 'Saturdays of Souls' when the dead are commemorated) with the vision of victory of the Tatars in 1380, and of his own death, received by Prince Dimitri on his name-day during the singing of the hymn to the

Theotokos, 'It is meet, in truth to bless thee . . .' at the end of the consecration in the Liturgy:

> Prince Dimitri was rapt in contemplation, his spiritual eyes were opened, and he beheld a marvellous vision: he sees not the candles burning before the icons nor the gems sparkling on the gold cases of the images, he hears not the sacred chanting: he sees the open plain, the open plain of Kulikovo. The plain is strewn with corpses of Christians and Tatars: the Christians glimmer like candles, and the Tatars are like black pitch. Over the plain of Kulikovo walks the most holy Mother of God and behind her come the Apostles of the Lord, the holy archangels and angels, with brightly burning candles. They are chanting the requiem over the relics of the Orthodox warriors.

'Holy Russia' is a frequently repeated theme, as when Fedor Tyutchev (1803–1873) surveys the poor villages and the humble landscape and declares, 'Weighed down by the burden of the cross, the King of Heaven, in the likeness of a servant, has walked up and down all of you, my native land, blessing you.'

The poem 'Trinity', a love poem published in 1827, attributed to Alexander Pushkin and based on a verse by Voltaire, expresses the intellectual's disdain for church doctrine while using it to deliver a compliment to a Princess Urúsova:

> 'The Three-in-One,' the Church says
> '– that's what God is.'
> I'd doubts: a triple god seemed past belief.
> Now, seeing you, I've faith. What relief!
> I can adore three Graces in one goddess.

Maksimilian Voloshin's (1877–1932) poem 'Holy Russia', written in 1917, points to what Russians have squandered in forsaking the Tsar and accepting the enemy, but he is unable to condemn:

Shall I dare cast a stone at you? Shall I condemn your wild and passionate flame? Shall I not bow down before you with my face in the mud, blessing the trace of your bare foot, you homeless, wanton, drunken Russia – fool in Christ!

Lermontov takes some doctrinal liberties when, in his poem 'The Angel', the heavenly being who sings of the great God and of 'the bliss of innocent spirits in the shade of the gardens of paradise' is bringing from heaven a young soul 'destined for the world of sorrow and tears'. Nikolay Nekrasov (1821–1877) recounts the story of the penitent Vlas, who had been a violent bully but, seeing a vision of sinners in hell while lying on his sickbed, repented and vowed to build churches, so that he now walks through icy winters and summer heat entreating Christian Russia to give what it can:

Uncle Vlas, a grey-haired old man in a peasant's coat, with an open collar and with his head uncovered, slowly passes through the town. A copper icon hangs at his breast; he is collecting alms to build a godly church; he is hung with chains, poorly shod, with a deep scar on his cheek.

There is nostalgia for Holy Russia in the later poems of Anna Akhmatova (1889–1966), as when she summons up an image of white churches, the lighting of the lamps before the icons and the merry ringing of Christmas bells when 'men rejoice as angels do on God's Holy Day'. It is also to be found in Osip Mandelstam (1891–1938) as he evokes the polyphony of a girls' choir, a nun singing ancient chants and the five-domed cathedrals of Moscow 'with their Italian and Russian soul'.

One of the best-known and consistently Orthodox pieces is Count Aleksey Tolstoy's (1817–1875) poem *John Damascene*. It was set by Tchaikovsky's pupil and colleague Sergei Ivanovich Taneyev (1856–1915) as his Opus 1, a cantata for chorus and orchestra, entitled *St John of Damascus*, including a troparion that is a paraphrase of parts of the burial service.

What joy in this life has no part in earthly sorrow? Whose hope is not vain, and where among men is there one who is happy? All that we have acquired with effort is inconstant and worthless; what earthly glory stands firm and unchangeable? All is but ashes, phantom, shadow, and smoke, everything will vanish like the dust of a whirlwind, and we stand before death unarmed and helpless. The hand of the mighty is feeble, the commands of kings are as nothing. Receive, O Lord, Thy departed servant into Thy blessed habitations!

9

Fasting, confession and prayer

Baptism defines the life of the Orthodox Christian, though it may be something received in infancy and of which one has no conscious memory. Kallistos Ware quotes the words from the *Century*, a manual of Hesychast prayer by two fourteenth-century saints, Kallistos and Ignatios Xanthopoulos: 'The aim of the Christian life is to return to the perfect grace of the Holy and Life-giving Spirit, which was conferred upon us at the beginning in divine Baptism.' *The Sayings of the Desert Fathers*, wrote Metropolitan Anthony of Sourozh, has been for centuries an inspiration to those Christians who strove for an uncompromising obedience to the word and spirit of the gospel. He points out the insistent stress within the collection on ascetic endeavour and contrasts that with the modern desire for 'experience'. The modern person (he was writing in 1975) is placed at the centre of those things that he or she wishes to make subservient to this aim. God too, in this manner of living, becomes the source from which the highest experience flows, rather than the One whom we adore, worship and are prepared to serve at whatever cost to ourselves. Metropolitan Anthony always spoke and wrote in a way that made the content of the Christian faith both attractive and accessible, yet never diluted or diminished the gospel message. He presented asceticism as the necessary response to the God who in Christ taught us to renounce ourselves, take up our cross and follow Him. Human beings bear the imprint of God's image and so belong to God, to whom they must render what is due. No effort, no sacrifice is too great and that, teaches Vladyka Anthony, is the very basis of an ascetic understanding of life. It is at first rather surprising that he pointed to the desire for experiences more than forty years ago, as research into the preferences of today's younger generations suggests that they choose experiences rather than possessions; they would rather do something new and different than own something. This desire for experiences reaches its epitome in the so-called 'bucket list' (from the notion of death as 'kicking the bucket') – the things that one wants to do and the places to go before death. Asceticism – the spiritual, mental and physical discipline that enables a person to render to God what is due to God – is also directed towards death, but with the intention that, by the grace of God, human persons should have so lived this life that they will pass into eternal life. Vladyka Anthony did not think that we had to emulate the incredible feats of physical endurance of the Desert Fathers and Mothers, though he thought that there was much to be learned from their integrity, their unrelenting courage, their vision of God 'so Holy, so great, possessed of such love, that nothing less than one's whole being could respond to it'. The full rigour of the ascetic tradition can be studied in the paterika. In everyday Orthodoxy there are three particular disciplines: fasting, confession and prayer.

Orthodox fasting

It is simply not possible to be authentically Orthodox without adhering to some version of the fasting rules. There are four types of fast: fasting prior to receiving communion, the weekly fast on Wednesday and Friday, the Seasonal Fasts and the Great Lenten Fast.

Fasting prior to communion is the simplest. The eucharistic fast involves total abstinence from any food or drink in the morning prior to receiving communion, from going to bed the night before or at least from midnight. When, as on certain days in Lent, the Liturgy of the Presanctified Gifts may be offered in the evening, the fast is for the whole day or at least from noon. This is an essential preparation for receiving communion.

The weekly fast on Wednesdays and Fridays is observed every week except from Christmas Day to the eve of the Theophany, the week following the Sunday of the Publican and the Pharisee (this is the first week of Pre-Lent and meat is allowed every day, being given up in the next week), Bright Week (Easter Day to St Thomas Sunday) and Trinity Week (Pentecost to the Saturday before All Saints' Sunday). The three other extra fast days are the eve of the Theophany (5 January), the beheading of St John the Baptist (29 August) and the Elevation of the Cross (14 September). Each of these days is observed in two ways: by abstaining from certain foods and by having one main meal. On fast days, no meat, eggs, dairy products, fish, wine or olive oil are to be eaten (though there are some days in the calendar when fish is allowed). One meal a day is eaten, towards evening (that is, after Vespers).

The Seasonal Fasts occur prior to Christmas, on the Feast of the Apostles at the end of June and the Dormition of the Theotokos. The Nativity Fast (also called St Philip's Fast) is from 15 November until 24 December, that of the Apostles Peter and Paul from 11 to 28 June, and that of the Dormition of the Theotokos from 1 to 14 August. All dates are inclusive, and for those who follow the Julian Calendar the dates in the Civil Calendar will be 13 days later. These are all strict fasts with varying rules. During the Nativity Fast there is no oil or wine on Monday, Wednesday and Friday, and no fish on Thursday, when there can be oil and wine. Fish can be eaten on Saturday and Sunday except between 20 and 24 December inclusive. During the Apostles' Fast there is no oil or wine on Monday, Wednesday and Friday, and no fish on Thursday, when there can be oil and wine. Fish can be eaten on Saturday and Sunday. During the Dormition Fast wine and oil are allowed only on Saturdays and Sundays.

One of the surprising Orthodox practices is that it is possible to fast on a feast! This is not a new problem. Historically the Russians were somewhat surprised by the Greek rules on fasting, which turned more than half the year into fast days. Some embraced them to such a degree that they created ritualistic taboos, so that in some fast periods, according to ancient canons, infants could not suck from their mother's breasts! There were disputes over fasting in Russia in the twelfth century. Some, including some princes, wondered whether they had to fast on Wednesdays and Fridays when great church festivals such as Christmas fell on those days. In the

Greek Church local practice varied, so the Russian clergy had to find their own way. The general Russian custom in the twelfth century was more relaxed than the Greek: the fast was abolished on all great feast days. Two bishops of the city of Rostov, Nestor and Leo, set about reforming the rules. Nestor wanted to adopt the Greek practice and Leo required the strict fast on Wednesday and Friday regardless of what feast might fall on them. Prince Andrew Bogoliubsky proceeded energetically against the bishops, rather like the prince of Chernigov who, in 1168, deposed his bishop, Anthony, who 'forbade the prince to eat meat at dominical feasts'. It was clearly an objection that rumbled on through the centuries and on 25 June 1762 Tsar Peter III issued a decree to the Russian synod directing that the fasts of the Orthodox church year should no longer be obligatory for his subjects. Catherine the Great, by contrast, was a devout Orthodox Christian who fasted, went to confession, attended the Liturgy and received communion. All the fasting rules are subject to local variation caused by feasts with vigils and the local calendar indicates what is allowed or forbidden.

The 'Great Lent Fast' is really three linked fasts: Pre-Lent, Lenten and Great and Holy Week Fasts, with special rules for some specific days. To understand them it is necessary to know something about the calendar from Pre-Lent to Easter, which can be set out like this.

Pre-Lent: Sunday of Zacchaeus (*Slavic tradition*)
Week of normal fasting – that is, Wednesday and Friday
Sunday of the Publican and Pharisee (first Sunday of Pre-Lent)
Week of meat eating even on Wednesday and Friday
Sunday of the Prodigal Son (second Sunday of Pre-Lent)
Week of normal fasting – that is, Wednesday and Friday
Sunday of the Last Judgement: Meat-fare Sunday
*Week of no meat, but cheese, dairy products and eggs are allowed
even on Wednesday and Friday*
The Russian custom is to make visits and eat blini *(little pancakes)
during this week.*
Forgiveness Sunday: Cheese-fare Sunday (third Sunday of Pre-Lent)
Lent *begins on Monday*

First week: *Special rules for fasting*
Second to sixth week: *Strict fast*
Friday of sixth week: *Lent ends*
Saturday of Lazarus and Palm Sunday: *Special rules for fasting*
Great and Holy Week: *Strict fast with variations*

Pre-Lent moves from there being no fast from meat through prohibition on meat, and from unlimited dairy and eggs to no meat, dairy or eggs. Kallistos Ware helpfully explains that on the weekdays of Lent, Monday to Friday inclusive, there are restrictions on both the *number* of meals and the *types of food* permitted but, when a meal is allowed, there is no fixed limitation on the *quantity* of food to be eaten (his emphasis). The differentiation between number of meals, types of food and quantity is helpful. It will be seen that, though the bishop says there is no limitation on quantity, he does suggest small amounts where a person cannot observe a total fast but, by the same token, eating huge amounts of permitted types of food would go against the spirit of fasting.

The first week of Lent, beginning on Clean Monday (the day after Cheese-fare Sunday), is particularly strict. Ideally no food is eaten on Monday, Tuesday and Thursday, and one meal is eaten on each of the days Wednesday and Friday. If this is not possible, Monday is observed with a total fast, and bread and water (or tea or fruit juice) is taken after Vespers, but not a cooked meal. On Wednesday and Friday *xerophagy* is prescribed. The word literally means 'dry eating', which signifies vegetables cooked with water and salt, together with fruit, nuts, bread and honey. Other foods may be allowed (see below), but completely excluded are meat, animal products (cheese, milk, butter, eggs, lard, dripping), fish with backbones, olive oil and wine (and other alcoholic drinks). In the other weeks of Lent (Monday to Friday inclusive), one meal a day is permitted, after Vespers, and at this one meal xerophagy, as defined above, is to be observed. On Saturdays and Sundays in Lent, two main meals may be taken, one around midday and one in the evening, with wine and olive oil, but meat, animal products and fish are not allowed. Fish is permitted on Palm Sunday. There are some other variations concerning the Feast of the Annunciation and some other days that are too complicated to be included here. Most liturgical calendars will contain a note about fasting and the variations.

In Great and Holy Week there is one meal each day with xerophagy, though some try to keep a complete fast or to eat only uncooked food. On Holy Thursday one meal is eaten, with wine and oil. Great Friday is a total fast. Those unable to go without food for the whole day can eat bread with a little water, tea or fruit juice after the veneration of the Epitaphion at Vespers. In principle there is no meal on Holy Saturday, as the faithful stayed in church after the morning Liturgy, but in practice the faithful go home and there is a meal, when there may be wine, but no olive oil (the only Saturday on which oil is not allowed).

What fasting demands

In trying to answer the question of what precisely it is that the rules of fasting demand, Metropolitan Kallistos finds that in neither ancient nor modern times has there been exact uniformity. He also observes that often fasts are relaxed in practice, and not just for people who are elderly or in ill health. It is in the spirit of Orthodox ascesis that this should not be a personal judgement but something agreed with one's spiritual father. There are certainly plenty of conflicting views to be found on the web.

A strict view would be that a *fast* means *fasting* and not pretending to fast. Any relaxation should be granted by a person's spiritual father for specific reasons and times and should not undermine the principle of fasting. A strict approach would also hold that *oil* means all forms of oil, such as sunflower, rapeseed and so on, and not just olive oil. If that view is extended then all modern foods that are substitutes for prohibited foods could be disallowed, including, for example, soya products used instead of milk and vegetable margarine used instead of butter. Bishop Ware holds that *oil* means olive oil (which was also the view of the medieval Latin theologian Thomas Aquinas when asked if other oils could be substituted for olive oil in the sacrament of anointing). There is also a question of fish, as sea creatures without backbones, such as octopus and shellfish, are generally allowed when fish is prohibited. Russian writers have a tendency to say that Greeks are always looking for ways to break the fasting rules! However, it is somewhere recorded that at the Moscow Theological Academy and Seminary, at Holy-Trinity Sergius Lavra, students and staff would eat fish throughout Lent, twice in most weeks, though it used to be as often as four times. The diary of Tsar Nicholas II shows that the Imperial Family were served fish throughout Lent. There would certainly have been some justification for these dispensations from the rules, if only the Orthodox principle of economy.

Some writers, without being very strict in their approach, deplore the tendency to turn the Lenten question into the equivalent of 'Is it kosher?' The focus, they say, then shifts from the discipline of the body to the avoidance of certain ingredients for the sake of ritual purity, and food writers recommend recipes for good tasty food that satisfies the prohibitions of a fast but certainly does not keep to the spirit of fasting. There is a danger of Phariseeism in finding apparently legitimate ways to mitigate the effect of the rules, then in boasting about observing the fast while frustrating its purpose. It is equally wrong to add to the strictness of the fast, such as fasting on Monday in addition to Wednesday and Friday, without the agreement of a spiritual guide.

Some good practical advice for Lent is to be found in the writings of the martyred Russian priest Father Alexander Men, much of which is addressed to people making first steps in Orthodoxy after the Soviet persecution. He lays down seven general rules. The first is:

Abstaining from meat is a must. Any other rules can be discussed with a spiritual leader. In addition, it is good to choose a particular, everyday thing from which to abstain during these days, continuing until Pascha.

The other rules are (2) to read all the Gospels during Lent, (3) to refrain from all superfluous meetings and activities, (4) to read the

Prayer of St Ephrem of Syria every day and to meditate on it, (5) to dedicate at least ten minutes a day to prayerful meditation, (6) to keep silence for a period after each meditation, and (7) to attend the Liturgy every Sunday and to be on time!

Though Father Men does not insist on the full fast, his approach is anything but lax. Fasting is here part of a pattern of spiritual activity. If this approach were adopted in one year it is likely that a person would want to adhere more closely to the rules of fasting in subsequent years. As Bishop Ware also says, the two tendencies, overemphasizing the rules in a legalistic way or scorning them as outdated and unnecessary, both amount to a betrayal of true Orthodoxy.

Confession

As we have already seen, repentance is a key theme in Orthodoxy. Confession is a necessary part of repentance. Different churches within Orthodoxy approach confession in different ways, in terms of necessity, frequency and practice. All teach that repentance and with it confession of sin is necessary, and certainly essential if one has fallen into serious sin. If we compare practice, we will probably find that Russians have the highest expectations concerning confession, which is available at nearly every service, before, after and often during the office and Liturgy, and that the Greeks are more likely to have to make an appointment with the priest in order to make confession. Russians expect that someone who is going to receive communion will be fasting and will generally have made confession recently, that day or the evening before. A regular communicant will be guided by his or her spiritual father as to the necessary frequency of confession.

What can be seen in a Russian church is something like this. A priest emerges from behind the iconostasis, wearing the undercassock, the *podryasnik*, and gown, the *riassa*, and a stole, the epitrachelion. He will be carrying a book of the Gospels and a cross for kissing. He goes to one of the lectern-like stands and waits. Very soon someone will come to him and, remaining standing, will begin making confession. At a discreet distance a good-tempered queue may form. If a member of the choir or a server comes for confession, that person may go straight to the front. This is usual and expected; such individuals have ministries to perform. Confession may be very short or it may take some time. There may be conversation, discussion between priest and penitent, even, it seems, argument. At a word, the penitent bows, the epitrachelion is placed over his or her head, the words of forgiveness are pronounced and the sign of the cross made on the covered head; the stole, the Gospel Book and cross, and perhaps the hand of the priest, are kissed. As the penitent moves away, perhaps with joyful countenance, perhaps with tears, the next in line may bow to the one behind and go and join the priest. Sometimes the priest, indicating that someone should wait, goes back behind the screen, joins in singing and prayers, and then returns. There is no impatience, nor is there any sense that confession should be hidden. All have sinned, and all need repentance, confession and forgiveness.

'Father,' asks a convert new to the practice of confession, 'what do you expect from me in my confession?' 'Whatever you want to say,' comes the reply. The rite for confession itself states, in the words of the priest to the penitent, that Christ stands there invisibly and receives the confession. So the penitent need not be anxious or afraid, but also must not conceal anything that should be confessed, for that would be a greater sin. Only when the faithful have confessed can they receive forgiveness. Coming to the Great Physician, the penitent should want to be healed and nothing should stand in the way of the healing, of which the priest is merely the minister. In preparing for confession the penitent is certainly looking for individual acts and omissions, but is also looking for a wrong spirit. As already seen, the prayer of St Ephrem the Syrian, said throughout Great Lent, asks God first to remove the spirit of sloth, despair or vain curiosity, lust of power or ambition and idle talk, and then to give in its place the spirit of chastity or soberness, humility, patience and love. To this is added a prayer that the faithful should see their own faults, failures and transgressions rather than those of other people. Confession before a priest continues the process that takes place day by day in prayer. The confession in the order for Daily Prayer identifies the possibilities for sin. These are found in deeds, words, thoughts, and in indulging the senses. It also understands that people sin both willingly and unwillingly and both knowingly and unknowingly, and that some sins are visible and others are hidden. A penitent might use a list to search out sins, and there are plenty of these lists of questions to the penitent to be found on the web, often prepared by parish clergy to aid parishioners who ask how they should prepare for confession. They used to be the basis of questions asked of the penitent by the priest. Lists always carry the drawback that they may make suggestions for sin that you would never have thought of otherwise. They can also give rise to a scrupulosity – a fear that one has forgotten to confess everything – that is obsessive–compulsive and bad for psychological and spiritual health.

The prayers preparatory to receiving communion tell us something about what the Orthodox Christian is to confess. We are, they say, defiled by 'unbecoming works': that is to say, works unbecoming of a Christian, called elsewhere 'unseemly deeds'. They teach that it is the passions, uncontrolled desires and false beliefs, such as that material possessions will increase our happiness, that give rise to what is unbecoming or unseemly. St Tikhon of Zadonsk (1724–1783), Bishop of Voronezh, in his book on *The Mystery of Holy Repentance*, taught that Christians should consider whether they live in a way that is worthy of the gospel and should look at 'how we live, how we conduct ourselves, how we think, how we talk, how we act, with what kind of heart we go before the God who sees all things [and] how we treat one another'. Confession is intended as an aid to salvation and a source of spiritual health. By receiving the sacraments devoutly, Christians continue the work done when they were baptized and Chrismated, a work that restores the wedding garment, removing the stains, cleaning and refurbishing it. The urgent desire of Christians is to be ready when the Bridegroom comes and not to be left outside the bridal chamber of Christ. As we saw earlier, the Church's worship gives the language that is needed for this, which Christians make their own as they pray,

Make the robe of my soul to shine, O Giver of Light and save me . . . Strip from me the disfigurement of sin, through participation in Thy sufferings; clothe me in the glorious robe of Thy beauty, and in Thy compassion make me feast with joy at Thy Kingdom.

Prayer

The Orthodox Church teaches that those who would pursue a spiritual life, including fasting, confession and prayer, need spiritual guidance. Historically the Orthodox have sought and found this in monasteries, especially from such of the elders called to be a staretz. What takes place between a spiritual father and his children is generally hidden, but some have written letters of guidance which have been shared. One such was Staretz John of Valamo, a Russian monk canonized by the Ecumenical Patriarch in 2018. As a consequence of the Russian Revolution, he lived more than half his life in Finland. He died in 1958 and is buried in the graveyard at New Valamo. He wrote many letters of guidance to his spiritual children, among them two Russian women who lived in Helsinki, who kept the staretz's letters. They attended St Nicholas's Church, Helsinki, which was then considered an outpost of traditional real Russian Orthodoxy. It was to their apartment that Archimandrite (now Metropolitan) Panteleimon went when beginning to write his book about Father John, *A Star in the Heavens*. He describes the experience as that of stepping into a distinctly Russian world. Everything was exactly as it should be in a Russian household, perhaps in Leningrad. The living room was crowded with things: furniture, tables, chairs and two large beds. Paintings large and small hung on the walls, together with innumerable small framed photographs, all in a pleasing state of disorder. As the old women were devoutly Orthodox, one corner contained a great number of icons of all ages and depicting a variety of subjects. The apartment was furnished in the Russian style, in a state of carefree but comfortable disarray. Gone, writes the Archimandrite, was the systematic cold atmosphere of the Western world, and in its place was the human warmth of this Eastern people. In the middle of the room was a dining table with chairs arranged around it, in the Russian style: some fine antique ones interspersed with a few standard post-war specimens. In due course a meal would be served, also in the Russian fashion – a large number of dishes, sweet and savoury, meat, fish, vegetables, hot and cold, all placed on the table, with bottles and glasses in various sizes – and the meal would last many hours.

The apartment, furniture and meal reveal an underlying culture, and that same culture is found in Orthodox spirituality that has a Russian flavour. Precisely because of the stress on having a spiritual father, usually a monastic elder, rather than following a general spiritual method set out in books, the person seeking to pursue a spiritual life will receive advice and guidance that is personal and specific, while reflecting the spiritual genealogy of the staretz. The Church cannot produce *startsi* to order. As John of Valamo observed, one studies for the priesthood, but one is born to be a staretz. The staretz listens to the person who comes to him, guides, consoles and encourages, and this listening is more than just hearing words spoken, it is a reading of the person's spiritual state, for the staretz hears the inner voice too. Igumen Chariton, last abbot of the old Valamo and first abbot of the New, explained in the foreword to his anthology *The Art of Prayer* (written in Russian in 1936 and published in English thirty years later) that he had been guided as a zealous young monk by his staretz, who continually solved the perplexities he encountered in the practice of the Jesus Prayer. He says that after the death of his staretz he was 'forced to have recourse to the writings of wise Fathers'. From these writings he drew out all that was essential concerning the Jesus Prayer, wrote it in a notebook and so, year by year, developed an anthology on prayer. It was intended to be a personal resource, a help with prayer. It had no systematic order and themes were frequently repeated. The major source was the writings of Theophan the Recluse, but there are extracts and sayings from the Desert Fathers, from John Cassian, Gregory Palamas, Ephraim the Syrian and Barsanuphius, as well as from Nil Sorski, Paisius Velichkovsky, Ignatius Brianchaninov and John of Kronstadt. The sources are somewhat disordered, mixed in antiquity and in relative value, yet combined in a way that is homely and comforting while enunciating a spirituality that seems genuinely attainable.

John was born in 1873 and entered Valamo in 1889. From 1893 until 1897 he did military service in the Tsarist army and only returned to Valamo in 1900. He joined the brotherhood in 1907 and became a monk in 1910. In the extraordinary year 1921 he was ordained both hierodeacon and hieromonk and sent to be abbot of St Tryphon monastery in Petsamo on the Arctic coast of Finland. In 1932 he returned to Valamo, to the skete of St John the Baptist, and became a schema-monk. He was the monastery's confessor from 1938, moving with the brotherhood when it was evacuated early in 1940. He reposed at New Valamo in 1958. His published spiritual letters begin in August 1939. In them he tells that they left the old monastery hurriedly as the Soviet army advanced; he regretted that some icons were left hanging on the wall of his cell, but, he wrote, 'I took a few books of the Holy Fathers, and that is enough.' He says of himself, 'I was not educated,' yet he was well read in the Fathers, the early ascetics and the *Philokalia* (the Russian version, first printed in 1793, was entitled *Dobrotoliubie*) being his favourite reading.

The book of letters, *God is in Our Midst*, takes its title from his most frequently used salutation, that with which the concelebrating priests exchange the peace during the Liturgy. Each letter is a response to someone who has asked for his spiritual guidance, some of whom visited him at New Valamo. He describes himself as ignorant, with no spiritual experience of his own and always borrowing from the Holy Fathers, but he cannot actually disguise the real depth of his spiritual insight which shows through in every letter. His spirituality was shaped by what he read as well as by what he practised. 'In our time,' he says, 'we are not blessed with the possibility of living under the guidance of a staretz experienced in the spiritual life. A guide should show you the way he himself has gone.' John was a very zealous youth, but he could not find holy ascetic men and did not meet a teacher who would support his zeal and give him proper spiritual guidance. He clearly regrets this. In an undated letter written towards the end of his life, he thanks his correspondent for the gift of an icon of St Seraphim of Sarov, but says that it causes him to look at the saint's life and to examine his own empty life: 'It is terrible; sometimes I am ready to tear my hair for my negligence.' Yet in reading that heartfelt line we might think of another in which he writes, 'the closer a person comes to God, the more sinful he sees himself to be'.

The letters were not written for publication, though he did not prohibit it, and he was not setting out to write a spiritual textbook or an anthology such as that of Igumen Chariton. There are, how-ever, some forty named sources in the letters and on a number of occasions he refers to a book, saying something like 'p. 187, chap. 23, 10th line from the top' or telling his correspondent to miss out certain pages or passages. John Climacus is cited fourteen times, Isaac the Syrian eleven times, Barsanuphius nine times, Maximus the Great six times, Peter Damascene five times, John Cassian and Abba Dorotheos four times each. He also recommends the book *Unseen Warfare*, written by a Catholic priest, Lorenzo Scupoli of the Theatine Order, which was published in Venice in 1549, then edited by Nicodemus of the Holy Mountain and revised by Theophan the Recluse. He also quotes Seraphim of Sarov, Ignatius Brianchaninov, John of Kronstadt and the Optina-startsi, the elders of the Optina monastery, whom he describes as 'steeped in the spir-it of the Holy Fathers'. His preference for the Fathers is clear; to one correspondent he writes: 'After reading the books of the Holy Fathers, of course you find Bishop Theophan's books dry. They can be compared this way: the Holy Fathers' writings are cream, and Bishop Theophan's are skimmed milk with water added.' Father John's spiritual genealogy shows a clear line of descent from the early ascetics through the later mystics to the systematizers; each part of his spiritual DNA shows through in a practical approach to spirituality. 'We must exert ourselves,' he writes. 'It helps little if we only read and ask how to be saved.'

In the spiritual life, he teaches, there are three grades – begin-ners, intermediates and the perfect. One of the early mistakes that people make is to count themselves as intermediate when still a be-ginner. He thinks that, for all practical purposes, we can ignore the perfect. Matching the grades are three degrees of prayer: oral prayer, which is pronounced with the lips, though the mind strays; the prayer of the mind, in which the mind is enclosed in the words of the prayer and so does not stray; and the mental prayer of the heart, which is a reward of the deepest humility.

The beginner must make a start. He tells many of his correspondents that prayer is the most difficult of spiritual exercises and always, to the last breath, involves the labour of hard struggle. The beginner needs a rule for private prayer. It should be set according to the time available. Father John advises against taking on too much, especially at the beginning, and becoming a slave to the rule or else rushing prayer in order to get through it all. A person should determine the rule him or herself and then try to pray attentively. There are many possible methods, for some of the Fathers practised inner prayer of the mind and prospered in the spiritual life, while others read many psalms, canons and troparions, and also prospered. Nevertheless, John favours inner prayer. He tells one correspondent, 'it is a good and saving thing that you force yourself to pray', and another, 'make yourself pray inwardly more often as far as you have strength and time'. Suggesting frequent reading of the Gospels, he observes that Holy Scripture is more important than canons.

The chief work in the spiritual life is prayer. Attentiveness is the soul of prayer. The active mind needs to be contained in the words of the prayer and attention needs to descend from the head to the upper part of the chest (he says not to push it to the heart). It is difficult at first, but becomes easier to achieve. It is unnecessary to seek for anything else, such as warmth in prayer. Should it come, then the one praying should stop and stay with it until it passes. One should not strive for it for oneself. One should strive for the one thing that is needful, and all the rest will be added. Of course Staretz John commends the Jesus Prayer in the form, 'Lord Jesus Christ, Son of God, have mercy on me, a sinner', but also says, 'you can pray in other words as it suits you best'. Recommending to one correspondent a hundred repetitions of the Jesus Prayer morning and evening, he stresses that our part in prayer is work and that the rest is grace – 'seek nothing more and do not get excited. In the spiritual life there is no place for leaps; what is required is patience.' When some complain of dryness or lack of progress, he says simply, 'Go on praying as you are now.' It is a basic teaching of his that the Lord gives prayer to the one who prays.

Responding to the problems and difficulties of his correspondents, some of whom were nuns, Staretz John establishes the necessary preconditions for effective prayer. He defines this as a pure conscience towards God, people and things. For a pure conscience towards God, one must try to fulfil the gospel commandments. By these he means those such as 'judge not, that ye be not judged', 'do not do to others what you would not have them do to you', 'be reconciled with your adversary', 'forgive and you will be forgiven'. For a pure conscience towards people, one must try not to condemn people or to be hostile. He warns against condemning anyone for anything and warns that 'the Lord does not hear prayer where there is hatred'. For a pure conscience towards things, one must use things without attachment.

Father John points out that the spiritual life is complicated, that it requires deep humility and cannot be understood by reason. It is grasped only by experience, when one tries to live in accordance with the counsels of the Holy Fathers. He is less concerned about bodily passions than about the passions of the soul, which he lists as envy, rancour, arrogance, slyness, hypocrisy, flattery and greed for money. The spiritual life is not all progress. 'At a time of trouble,' he advises, 'wait for peace, and when there is peace prepare for trouble. In this temporal life peaceful and troubled phases alternate. Even the holy men of God were not free from these changes.' The important thing when we fall is to get up, and if we fall again to get up again. It is humankind's characteristic to fall, but the Devil's is not to repent. The only deadly sins are those of which we are aware yet do not repent of them. Sorrows will come; we may become depressed and faint-hearted. The Fathers also experienced this. Without humiliating events we do not become humble. It is the Devil who brings despair, and we must not listen to him.

Three things are necessary: the Holy Scriptures, the Holy Fathers and prayer. He recommends the lives of the saints as 'very inspiring for us sinners'. In commending the Fathers he also warns us not to assume that we will understand them. Some can only be understood by people genuinely leading a spiritual life. The language of Isaac the Syrian is particularly difficult but, says Staretz John, using a striking image, 'it is still more difficult for us to understand the content, for the well is deep and our rope is short and we cannot reach his deep, wonderful, saving water'. We do not find much about confession and communion here because, as we can see from the letters, his correspondents are already regular in both these things, though not always happy with their clergy. Father John has some sympathy with them and prays, 'Lord, grant me to see my own sins and not to judge the priests.'

Staretz John rarely tells someone what to do. He suggests, explains and encourages; he occasionally tells people that they are being silly or wanting in sense. He warns someone that what he or she is striving for is the mode of life proper for monastic hermits, which requires complete freedom from cares. His correspondent is occupied all day with cares and troubles, with the worldly life of vanities. One has to adapt oneself to the life as it is. He tells another that her conceit and vainglory stop her from seeing herself as she really is, and refuses to accept another letter from someone until she is reconciled to one she says she hates. To many he says, 'The Lord give you wisdom,' and he tells someone not to accept his advice if he or she feels that it is inconsistent with the Holy Scriptures and with the message of the Holy Fathers. He generally finishes his letters with tender words, such as 'the Lord keep you, my spiritual child'.

John of Valamo embodies and expresses the Orthodox spiritual tradition that was heavily influenced by the asceticism of the early monks and hermits, a tradition that passed from the Desert Fathers of Egypt through Palestine and Mount Athos to Constantinople and from there to Kiev, so to shape 'the Russian religious mind'. As a monk, he participates in the tradition and, as a staretz, he transmits it in a way that makes it relevant for the modern age, applying it in specific personal situations. Like the Helsinki apartment where some of his letters were received, we find here vital human warmth, but this warmth comes from the Spirit as the reward for a life of spiritual struggle.

10

The resurrection life

In the 7024th year [1515] at daybreak, after they had celebrated the Nativity of the all-glorious Theotokos, as the day of the Resurrection of our Lord God and Saviour Jesus Christ was dawning [that is, Sunday], the ninth day of September, on the memorial of the holy righteous ancestors of God Joachim and Anne, while the [great] doxology was being sung, father passed away and surrendered his honourable soul to God with three final breaths, signifying with the three breaths the holy and life-creating Trinity. The brothers began to sing the 'Holy God' [Trisagion] from the chant for the departure of a soul, every man shedding many tears. They dressed his long-suffering body in burial clothes and, lifting him up over their heads, they carried him into the church, as the stalwart sons of the patriarch Jacob had done of old. They did not sing joyful songs, but lamentations.

In these words of monk Dosifej, included in the Volokolamsk Paterikon, we learn of the death of the Venerable Hegumen Iosif. The funeral oration points to great grief experienced by the brotherhood on being so deprived of a father and experienced pastor; 'the venerable one has been removed from his flock, the blessed one has stepped out of the sheepfold and the sheep sorely grieve'. The brothers grieve for their loss rather than for their hegumen and Dosifej tells them that it is proper already to leave off lamentations. The word 'lamentations' refers back from the death and burial of an individual to Christ Himself being laid in the tomb. At the end of Vespers on Holy Friday, a procession of the Epitaphion takes place. In the Greek tradition, it takes place as this aposticha is sung:

Down from the Tree Joseph of Arimathea took Thee dead, who art the Life of all; and he wrapped Thee, O Christ, in a linen cloth with spices. Moved in his heart by love, he kissed Thy most pure body with his lips; yet, drawing back in fear, he cried to Thee rejoicing: 'Glory to Thy self-abasement, O Thou who lovest mankind'.

In the Russian tradition, it happens during the troparion, 'Noble Joseph, taking down Thy most pure body from the Tree, wrapped it in clean linen with sweet spices, and he laid it in a new tomb.' The lamentation over Christ's tomb is the source of that over Iosif's corpse; it is the grief of those who have had the one they love removed from them, the shepherd taken from the sheepfold. Jesus was profoundly aware of what His friends would feel when, in the farewell discourses, He spoke to them gently, acknowledged their grief and promised them that they would not be left comfortless. The Church's lament is already ambivalent, for a note of joy and of triumph creeps into it. At Holy Saturday Mattins, a funeral hymn is sung, a song at Christ's burial, not in lament but because, 'by Thy burial Thou hast opened for me the gates of life'. A very similar tension to the one we found between the One and the Three in the Holy Trinity is found now between death and life, as the kontakion declares, 'as a corpse the Immortal is wrapped in linen with sweet spices and laid in a tomb'. The tomb is called 'happy' that receives within itself the Creator as one asleep. Again the cry is heard: 'O strange wonders!' Mattins concludes:

> We venerate Thy Passion, O Christ.
> We venerate Thy Passion, O Christ.
> We venerate Thy Passion, O Christ, and Thy
>   Holy Resurrection.

As Vespers of Holy Saturday progresses, praise takes over from lament, for 'The Lord has waked as if from sleep.' The full joy of Easter is not yet come. A little before Paschal Mattins begins, a short time before midnight, the choir is still singing a funeral hymn, the canon of Holy Saturday. The Easter procession, the one so eagerly awaited outside the cathedral in Paris's rue Daru in Lesley Blanch's narrative, emerges from the temple preceded by lanterns and, with the faithful carrying lighted candles, makes its way around the outside of the building in a slow and dignified fashion. The choir sings slowly the verse, 'Thy Resurrection, O Christ the Saviour, is sung by the angels in heaven and also by us on earth; make us worthy to glorify Thee with a pure heart.' Before the closed west doors the priest will proclaim that Christ is risen from the dead, 'by death having conquered death, and having given life to those that were in the grave'. Now the sure unsullied joy of the Resurrection falls on the Church as she cries out, 'Christ is risen!'

The services of Holy Thursday, Holy Friday, Holy Saturday and Easter Day, the Pascha, model the spiritual journey of Orthodox Christians. John of Valamo urges his spiritual children to be aware of death. Remembrance of death, he writes, is a gift of God, and he recalls that somewhere, but he doesn't know where, it says, 'Remember your end and you will sin no more.' He teaches that this temporal life is the path to eternity and our preparation for it. He is clear that it is characteristic of human nature to fear death, and calls St Maximus the Confessor and St John Climacus as witnesses. Early in January 1949 he wrote to someone who had been present at the death of their mother, having never before seen someone die. It is his experience that deaths differ; he tells of Igumen Mavrikki of Valamo who struggled with death for forty days, and priest-monk Irenei for sixty days, but also describes how, just the day before, they had buried a seventy-four-year-old monk who died suddenly. 'Before dinner,' Staretz John writes, 'he was working; after dinner he stayed in his cell alone. When they came to his cell, he was lying by the table, having given his soul to God.' Death is inevitable and the manner of death differs, but all will in a sense die. Father John continues:

> Man does not die, but moves into another, eternal life. The body is of earth and goes into the earth, but the soul is of God and goes to God. That is his holy will: to appoint each person

to eternal life according to his deeds. Lord, let Thy mercy be upon us, for our hope is in Thee.

It may seem surprising that he writes not 'faith', but 'deeds'. Orthodoxy teaches, as we have seen, that the grace of the Holy Spirit conferred when a person is baptized into the Holy Trinity is sufficient for the return to the original and natural human state of paradise. It is self-will and the passions, more the passions of the soul than of the body, that diminish that sufficiency. The wedding garment provides a powerful image of our spiritual state and the Church guides the faithful in many ways to ensure that the stains of sins are expunged. Orthodox scholar John Anthony McGuckin describes what he calls 'the fundamental bulwarks of the Orthodox faith' as the lives of the Spirit-filled elect, the Holy Scriptures, the ancient traditions found in liturgy and ritual, the creeds and professions of the ecumenical councils, the great patristic writings opposing heresies, the collection of prayers that have been universally adopted and found to be spiritually efficacious, the spiritual and ascetical writings of the saints, the significant statements of hierarchs in the more recent past. This list reflects the real life of the Church. It begins with Christians, the faithful Orthodox so often mentioned in the prayers, who are filled with the Spirit, who hear and absorb the Scriptures, who participate in the liturgies and rituals, who pray using hallowed words and who profess the faith in words shaped by the councils; they are likely to be aware of at least some of the Fathers and some of the ancient and modern saints from reading books, listening to homilies, keeping feast days and venerating icons, and may have some knowledge of statements issued by the hierarchy in response to events not anticipated by the councils. The faithful are the fundamental bulwark, the bedrock of Orthodoxy. Much effort therefore goes into guiding and encouraging them with the purpose that they should by all means be enabled to receive that which Christ has promised. The whole of Great Lent models the effort that is required, the struggle that is described by so many spiritual guides, as Great and Holy Week takes the faithful on a liturgical, sacramental and spiritual journey through the grave to the joy of Resurrection.

The Church is the community of the Resurrection. Easter is its centre and its aim. If its joy is in any way diminished it is because it carries too the knowledge of failure. It is to be found in the paterika, which are the lives not simply of those who succeeded in the spiritual struggle but also of those who failed and, better still, of those who went astray and then by penitence returned to the way of life. The liturgical texts of the Sunday of Pascha are laden with joy and with exhortation. 'Let us purify our senses and we shall behold Christ, radiant with the unapproachable light of the Resurrection . . .' 'Yesterday I was buried with Thee, O Christ, and today I arise with Thine arising.' 'Bearing lights let us go forth to meet Christ . . .' 'It is the day of Resurrection; let us be radiant for the festival, and let us embrace one another.' The words of John Climacus, like those of Cyril of Jerusalem to his newly enrolled catechumens, must be heard and heeded before one puts on radiance for the festival. He said, 'Never be overly confident, until you hear the final judgment against yourself', and it could be said that the very point of the great cycle of fast and feast is that by it the faithful are made ready both for the dread judgement at which they will give 'a good defence' and for the festival at which the chant learned on earth will be repeated in heaven with the angelic choir.

Let us who have beheld the Resurrection of Christ worship our holy Lord Jesus, Who is alone without sin. We worship Thy Cross, O Christ, and we praise and glorify Thy holy Resurrection. For Thou art our God, and we know none other beside Thee, and we call upon Thy Name. Come, all ye faithful, let us worship Christ's holy Resurrection, for behold, through the Cross joy hath come to the whole world. For ever blessing the Lord, we praise His Resurrection. He endured the Cross for us, and by death destroyed death.

Appendix 1

The Orthodox church year, the Paschalion and vestment colours

The calendar consists of a daily pattern of prayer, a weekly cycle of services, an annual cycle of moveable feasts centred on Easter, and the annual cycle of fixed feasts, commencing on 1 September. The Old Calendar dates are currently thirteen days behind the New Calendar, so, for example, the Exaltation of the Cross, 14 September, is celebrated on 27 September. Fixed dates are given Old Style/New Style. Some dates are fixed and some are moveable depending on the date of Easter. The date of Orthodox Easter (Paschalion) in the civil calendar (New Style) is as follows:

19 April 2020
2 May 2021
24 April 2022
16 April 2023
5 May 2024
20 April 2025
12 April 2026
2 May 2027
16 April 2028
8 April 2029
28 April 2030

It is the same as Latin Easter in 2025 and 2028 and a month apart in 2021, 2024 and 2027. Otherwise it is generally a week after Latin Easter.

The year begins on 1/14 September

8/21 September	The Nativity of the Theotokos
14/27 September	The Exaltation of the Cross
Sundays after Pentecost *continue*	
15/28 November	Beginning of the Nativity Fast
21 November/4 December	Presentation of the Theotokos in the Temple
Sunday before the Nativity of Christ	
25 December/7 January	The Nativity of Christ
1/14 January	The Circumcision of Christ
Sunday before the Theophany	
6/19 January	The Holy Theophany (Epiphany) The Baptism of Christ
Sundays after Pentecost *continue*	
2/15 February	The Meeting of Our Lord in the Temple *(Presentation/Purification)*
25 March/7 April	The Annunciation *(which will certainly fall in Lent or Great Week)*

Pre-Lent

Sunday of Zacchaeus *(Slavic tradition)*
Sunday of the Publican and the Pharisee
Sunday of the Prodigal Son
Sunday of the Last Judgement *(Meat-fare Sunday)*
Sunday of Forgiveness *(Cheese-fare Sunday)*

Great Lent begins

First Sunday in Lent	The Sunday of Orthodoxy
Second Sunday in Lent	St Gregory Palamas
Third Sunday in Lent	The Adoration of the Cross
Fourth Sunday in Lent	St John Climacus
Fifth Sunday in Lent	St Mary of Egypt
The Saturday of Lazarus	
Palm Sunday	
Holy and Great Monday	
Holy and Great Tuesday	

Holy and Great Wednesday
Holy and Great Thursday
Holy and Great Friday
Holy and Great Saturday

Pascha

Bright Week
Second Sunday of Pascha   Thomas Sunday
Third Sunday of Pascha   Sunday of the Myrrh-bearers
Fourth Sunday of Pascha   Sunday of the Paralysed Man
Fifth Sunday of Pascha   Sunday of the Samaritan Woman
Sixth Sunday of Pascha   Sunday of the Blind Man
Ascension of the Lord   Thursday of the sixth week
Seventh Sunday of Pascha   Sunday of the Holy Fathers of the First Ecumenical Council, AD 325
Trinity Saturday of Ancestors
Eighth Sunday of Pascha   Day of the Holy Trinity; Pentecost
Monday of eighth week   Day of the Holy Spirit
First Sunday after Pentecost
6/19 August   The Transfiguration of the Lord
15/28 August   The Dormition of the Theotokos

Colour of vestments

This information (which is not comprehensive) comes from Igumen Gregory Woolfenden's book *A Practical Handbook of Divine Services* (Jordanville, New York: Holy Trinity Publications, 2011) and conforms to Volume 4 of *The Handbook for the Clergy*, published in Moscow in 1983.

Light blue   Feasts of the Most Holy Mother of God (Nativity, Protection, Entering into the Temple, Annunciation, Falling Asleep) Meeting of the Lord (or white)
Claret or violet   Exaltation of the Holy Cross Sunday of the Veneration of the Holy Cross

Claret or red	Beheading of St John the Forerunner
White	St John the Theologian
	Eve of the Nativity of Christ
	Synaxis of the Most Holy Mother of God (or light blue)
	Circumcision of the Lord
	Theophany Great
	Saturday (after the Epistle in the Liturgy and until the end of Mattins on the first day)
	Ascension of the Lord
	Nativity of St John the Forerunner
	Transfiguration
Gold	Nativity of Christ (or white)
Violet or gold	Sundays of preparation for the Great Fast
Violet, crimson or black	Great Fast (weekdays)
	Liturgy of the Presanctified Gifts
Violet	Saturdays and Sundays of the Great Fast
	Feasts on weekdays of the Fast of Polyeleos rank
Green or white	Entry of the Lord into Jerusalem
Black or dark	Great and Holy Week
Violet	Great Thursday (or red)
Red	Pascha (until the leave-taking inclusive)
Green	Pentecost (Trinity Sunday)
	Monday of the Holy Spirit (or white)
Gold	Lesser feasts of the Lord on weekdays and Sundays outside Lent

Other colour schemes for vestments exist among the various Orthodox churches.

Appendix 2
An Orthodox glossary

Accidie
A technical term in asceticism indicative of sadness, spiritual torpor, sloth, despondency and a distaste for life. It was fully analysed by Evagrios Ponticus in the fourth century.

Acheiropoieton
An icon that has not been made by human hand but has appeared miraculously.

Aër (Slavonic *vuzdukh*)
The largest of the three veils used to cover the chalice and asterisk during the Liturgy. It represents the shroud of Christ. When the Creed is read or sung during the Liturgy, the priest shakes it over the chalice, symbolizing the descent of the Holy Spirit.

Agiasmos, see Holy Water

Akathistos, acathistus
Literally 'not sitting down'. Originally used for a Byzantine processional hymn, the word usually refers to a hymn sung in honour of the Theotokos. The hymn to the Virgin, comprising twenty-four stanzas, is divided into four parts, one sung on each of the first four Fridays of Great Lent. On the fifth Friday the whole hymn is sung in commemoration of the deliverance of Constantinople from the Avars and Slavs in 626. There are other akathists, including one addressed to the Most Sweet Jesus.

Altar

1 The sanctuary containing the Holy Table; easternmost area of the church, behind the screen

2 The Holy Table itself (Greek *hagia trapeza*, Slavonic *prestol*).

Ambo, ambon

A raised platform or elevated pulpit on the north side of the solea, in front of the iconostasis; the Gospel is chanted from here and it may be used for preaching. There is not generally an ambo in a Slavic church and the prayer described as 'behind the ambo' is said a little way west of the iconostasis, sometimes in front of the central analoy.

Analoy (Greek *analogion*)

A wooden stand with a sloping top on which is placed an icon or the Book of Gospels. It is often covered in fabric of the liturgical colour.

Anaphora

The Great Eucharistic Prayer. The central prayer of the Liturgy, beginning with the priest's greeting, 'Lift up your hearts'.

Anastasis

The Resurrection of Christ. The church in Jerusalem known to the Latins as the Holy Sepulchre is known by the Greeks as the Anastasis.

Antidoron

Literally 'instead of the gift'. The remains of the altar bread (prosphora), after the Lamb and particles have been removed, cut up and distributed at the end of the Liturgy; also bread that is blessed during the course of the Liturgy, but not consecrated. It is eaten immediately after communion (usually with warm, diluted wine) by those who have received communion and at the end of the service by those who have not received, as a sign of blessing and fellowship in Christ.

Antimension (Slavonic *antimins*)

Literally 'instead of a table'. The altar cloth, carrying scenes of the Passion and the Deposition from the Cross. Relics of the saints are sewn into it and it carries the signature of the bishop who has given the cloth for authorized celebration of the Eucharist. It was originally intended for use when there was no properly consecrated Holy Table, but is now always used in the manner of the Western corporal.

Antiphon

A selection from the psalms sung by alternating choirs. Also a psalm with a constant refrain sung after each verse. On Sundays they are now simply continuous psalms without the refrain.

Apodeipnon

Late evening service; Compline.

Apodosis (Slavonic *otdanive*)

The 'putting away' of a feast on the eighth day following (hence an 'octave'). The apodosis of Easter occurs after forty days, on the eve of the Ascension.

Apolytikon (Greek for 'dismissal')

The troparion or dismissal hymn, varying with the day or season, sung at the conclusion of Lauds and Vespers.

Apophthegm

The memorable saying of an 'old man', specifically the sayings of the Desert Fathers and Mothers in two collections, alphabetical and anonymous.

Apostle

1 One of the chief disciples of Christ.
2 The name given both to the passage from either the New Testament epistles or the Acts of the Apostles read during the Liturgy and to the book which contains the appointed readings.

3 The title 'Equal of the Apostles' is given to certain saints who contributed significantly to the spread of Christianity, such as Mary Magdalene, the Emperor Constantine and his mother Helena, Cyril and Methodius.

Archimandrite (Greek 'the ruler of a *mandra* or fold')

Originally a title for a monastic superior, now a title of honour for a member of the monastic clergy, who need not be the superior.

Archpriest

Title of honour; the highest rank a married priest can attain.

Artophorion

The tabernacle standing on the Holy Table in which the Blessed Sacrament is reserved.

Asterisk (Greek *asteriskos*, Slavonic *zvezditsa*, 'little star')

A utensil used in the Liturgy. It consists of two metal strips that each form an arch; they are held together by a central rivet, allowing them to swivel. When opened they form a frame placed over the bread on the diskos to prevent the veil disturbing the particles.

Autocephalous

The status of a national Orthodox Church which is self-governed, has the authority to elect or appoint its own head (patriarch or metropolitan) and can bless its own Chrism.

Autonomous

The status of a national Orthodox Church that is self-governing, but its governing hierarchy is appointed by a superior jurisdiction, usually a patriarch. An autonomous church may not be able to bless its own Chrism.

Axios

An exclamation made by the ordaining bishop and reiterated by the congregation, signifying that the person chosen is worthy to be ordained.

Bema

The chancel or sanctuary part of the church, usually at the east end.

Books, liturgical

Eight books are generally needed for services. Their names and content may differ between Greek and Slavic churches. They are the Gospel Book (*Evangelion*), the Book of Epistles (*Apostolos*), the Psalter (*Octoechos*), the *Triodion* and *Pentecostarion*, the *Menaion*, the *Horologion* and the service or liturgy book (*Euchologion* or *Ieratikon*).

Bread, the Holy

The square cut from the first prosphora at the Prothesis. It is called the Lamb and the Holy Bread both before and after consecration.

Calendar

The yearly system determining the arrangement of Orthodox feasts and fasts. The year begins on 1 September. Feasts are arranged according to the Old or Julian Calendar, which is now thirteen days behind the New or Gregorian Calendar, hence a feast will be shown as having two dates, one old, one new.

Candles (Greek *keri*)

Candles made of beeswax are used in Orthodox churches to express devotion to the Holy Trinity or the saints. They are also held or carried in various services or ceremonies and are seen as being symbolic of Christ, 'the Light of the World'.

Canon (Greek 'rule, standard')

1 The official list of books of the Bible recognized by the Church; these form the 'canonical Scriptures'. There are other historic

writings, such as the Protevangelium of James, that are not canonical, though they may have influenced some liturgical texts.

2 A poetic composition devised to fit specific liturgical occasions such as feast days. Generally made up of nine odes, the second of which is omitted except in Lent.

3 The rules or canons that guide the Church's discipline.

4 The Liturgical Canon refers to all the texts used for the Liturgy.

Cassock

1 The so-called 'inner cassock' (Greek *anteri* or *zostiko*; Russian *podryasnik*), with narrow sleeves, is worn by all clergy under their liturgical vestments. Monastics wear black, but married clergy wear a variety of colours, especially grey and blue.

2 The so-called 'outer cassock' – also called a *riassa* or *ryasa*, *exorason* or *rason* – which is black and has large sleeves, is worn over the inner cassock by clergy and monastics; it can be worn when celebrating a service such as Vespers, but is not worn beneath a sticharion. In the Greek tradition, chanters also wear it in church, without an inner cassock.

Cell

1 A hut or cave where a monk lives in the desert alone or with a disciple. A group of cells is called a lavra.

2 The room where a monk lives within a monastery.

Cenobium (Greek *koinos bios*, 'life in common')

A monastery where monks or nuns live a common life.

Censer (Greek *thymiato*, Slavonic *kadilo*)

A metal bowl with a detached lid, hung on chains, used for burning incense during services. The chains usually have bells attached, twelve in number, that represent the preaching of the Apostles.

Chalice (Greek *potirion*, Slavonic *vozduh*)

A large cup, symbolizing the vessel used at the Last Supper, usually of precious metal, on a long stem and broad base, and used at the Eucharist. It contains the wine that will become the Blood of Christ. Sufficient consecrated bread is added to it for communion to be given to the laity in both kinds using a spoon.

Chant (Greek *echos*, Slavonic *glas*)

The music proper to Orthodox services in the Byzantine tradition. There are eight tones or modes in Byzantine chant, which is chanted by chanters or cantors.

Chanter (Greek *psaltis*)

A lay person, who may wear an outer cassock, who chants the responses and hymns in (Greek) services. Chanters have to some extent been replaced by choirs.

Cherubic Hymn

The hymn sung at the Great Entrance; so called from the opening words, 'We, who mystically represent the Cherubim'. At the Vigil of Easter the hymn 'Let All Mortal Flesh Keep Silent' is sung instead, and at the Liturgy of the Presanctified 'Now the Hosts of Heaven'.

Chrism (Greek *myrron*)

Sanctified oil composed of several ingredients and fragrances used in the sacrament of Chrismation. It requires quite complex ceremonies for its consecration, taking about two weeks and concluding on the Thursday of Great Week. The right to consecrate Chrism does not belong to all Orthodox churches; some must get their supply from a higher body, such as a patriarch.

Communion cloth

A distinctive red cloth held beneath the mouth of those receiving communion, often by the deacon and a server, which is also used to wipe the mouth thereafter.

Compline (Greek *apodeinon*, Slavonic *velikoye povechaye*)

An office sung after dusk and often by monks in their cells. In the Slavonic tradition it is combined with Vespers and Mattins into the so-called All-Night Vigil. There are two forms, Great Compline used in Great Lent and Small Compline used at other times.

Crowns (Greek *stephana*, Slavonic *ventzy*)

Metal crowns or wreaths made of cloth, in the shape of lemon blossoms, used by the priest to 'crown' a couple during the sacrament of matrimony.

Cuffs, see Epikanikia

Curtain

A curtain may be drawn across the Holy Doors before and after and at certain points during the Liturgy, but it is not in universal use in Orthodoxy. It is generally drawn during the communion of the clergy and historically was closed after the Great Entrance and re-opened at the Creed.

Diakonikon (Greek 'place used by deacons')

An extension, usually on the south side of the sanctuary, used to house liturgical vestments, vessels and books.

Dikirotrikera

A set of two candleholders, one double-branched, the other triple-branched, used by a bishop to bless during the Liturgy. The dikerion signifies the two natures of Christ and the trikerion signifies the Holy Trinity. *See also* **Paschal trikerion**.

Diskos

The plate, the equivalent of the Western paten, on which the bread for the Eucharist is placed. It is generally larger than a paten, and deeper, and has a central foot. It is never placed on top of the chalice.

It is often engraved with scenes of the Nativity (the 'star', asterisk, being over it).

Dismissal

The formula with which an office is concluded.

Doxology (from Greek *doxa*, 'glory')

The act of giving glory to God, especially in prayer. The small form is, 'Glory to the Father and the Son and the Holy Spirit . . .' The Greater Doxology, sung during the All-Night Vigil and at the conclusion of Orthros, begins, 'Glory to God in the highest . . .'

Eagle (Greek *dikephalos aitos*, Slavonic *orletz*)

A small circular rug or a permanent design in the church floor, with a single-headed or double-headed eagle flying with outstretched wings over a city. It signifies the watchfulness and authority of the bishop over his diocese. The rugs are positioned at various places where the bishop will need to stand during the Liturgy.

Ecumenical Patriarch (Greek 'patriarch of the whole inhabited world')

Title borne by the Archbishop or Patriarch of Constantinople since the sixth century.

Eileton, *also* heileton

Literally 'something wrapped' or 'wound'. The silk cloth spread on the Holy Table during the Liturgy, with the antimension on top of it. It is slightly larger than the antimension and is folded around it at the conclusion of the Liturgy, when it is left on the Holy Table.

Ektene

A litany recited by the deacon (or a priest if there is no deacon), to which the choir responds, 'Lord, have mercy'. (*Ektenes* is an adjective meaning 'earnest', 'fervent'. It can also mean 'stretched-out'.)

Enarxis

Literally 'beginning'. The three antiphons and three prayers, with accompanying litanies, which form the introduction to the Liturgy.

Endyton

The second covering of the Holy Table, of bright and embroidered material.

Engolpion (Greek 'on the chest')

A medallion, usually of enamel and decorated with precious stones, which hangs on the chest of a bishop and signifies his episcopal office. A single engolpion is of the All-Holy Theotokos and is known as a Panagia. All primates and some bishops below the rank of primate have the dignity of a second engolpion, which usually depicts Christ.

Entrance

1 Little Entrance: the solemn procession of the clergy entering through the Holy Doors and carrying the Book of the Gospels.
2 Great Entrance: the transfer in procession of the Holy Gifts from the Proskomide to the Holy Table during the chanting of the Cherubic Hymn.

Epanokalymafko

The black monastic veil, representing the monk's death to the world, worn over the kalymafki and hanging down the back. Some Orthodox prelates of Slavic background, of metropolitan rank, wear a white epanokalymafko.

Eparchy (Greek 'province, region')

An area of ecclesiastical jurisdiction headed by a bishop, archbishop or metropolitan.

Epigonation (Greek from *epigounis*, 'thigh', Slavonic *palitsa* or *nabedrennik*)

A lozenge-shaped vestment formed of cardboard covered with cloth and decorated with a cross; it hangs from the right side. Worn by bishops, archimandrites and archpriests, it signifies, according to various accounts, the towel used to wipe the disciples' feet at the Last Supper and the 'sword of the Spirit'.

Epiklesis

The prayer in the Liturgy calling on the Holy Spirit to effect the consecration of the Holy Gifts.

Epimanikia (Slavonic *porutchi*)

Cuffs made of thickened fabric, usually embroidered with a cross, that lace on to the wrists of bishops, priests and deacons. Bishops and priests wear them over the sticharion and deacons wear them over the cassock sleeve.

Epiphany (Greek *theophania*, Slavonic *bogoyavleniye*)

The Orthodox Feast on 6/19 January commemorating the Baptism of Christ and the Manifestation of God the Holy Trinity. The Great Blessing of the Waters takes place on this day.

Epitaphion (Greek 'belonging to burial', Slavonic *plashchanitsa*)

A richly embroidered veil, on which is represented the scene of Christ's burial, carried in the procession at the end of Good Friday Vespers and at the end of the Orthros on Holy Saturday.

Epitrachelion (Greek 'about the neck')

The stole worn by an Orthodox priest when performing a sacrament. It is a long strip, fastened in front and decorated with crosses and a fringe. It is to be distinguished from the orarion of the deacon.

Euchologion (Greek 'book of prayers', Slavonic *sluzhebnik*)

A liturgical book used by the clergy and containing services, sacraments and prayers.

Exapostilarion (Greek 'despatching')

A hymn sung at Mattins after the canon that refers to Christ sending out His Apostles to preach to the whole world.

Exapterigia, *see* Fans

Exarch (Greek 'representative with full authority')

The head of an ecclesiastical jurisdiction, usually of the rank of archbishop or metropolitan, representing the head of the Church – that is, the patriarch. The Ecumenical Patriarchate has, for example, an exarchate of Russian parishes in Western Europe.

Fans (Greek *exapteriga*, Slavonic *rapidia*)

A light metal disc on a staff or pole bearing a representation of a six-winged Seraphim and representing the angels around the throne of God. Originally used to keep insects away from the Holy Gifts, they are now held by servers above the Book during the Gospel reading or above a special icon on a feast day.

Gerontikon (Greek *geron*, 'old man')

A book containing the life stories of the senior monks, the *gerontes*.

Girdle, *also* Zone (Greek *zone*)

The liturgical girdle is worn by priests and bishops over the sticharion; it is usually of the same colour as the phelonion. It passes through side openings in the sticharion and is fastened by a clasp or hook. It is not worn by deacons.

Great Church, the

The patriarchal cathedral church of Constantinople.

Hegumen, *also* igumen

Head of a monastic community; the equivalent of an abbot or prior.

Heirmos

Troparion at the beginning of each ode in a canon; in the original Greek composition it set the rhythmic pattern for singing. In any language its textual function is to provide a link between the biblical theme special to the ode and that of the celebration of which it is part.

High Seat

The bishop's throne in the centre of the wall of the apse behind the Holy Table.

Holy Gifts, Holy Things

The Oblation prepared during the Proskomide and so called both before and after consecration.

Holy Water (Greek *agiasmos*, Slavonic *sviataia voda*)

From the Greek for 'sanctification'. Water blessed during the 'Great Blessing' on the Epiphany or on some other occasion ('Small Blessing'), used for blessing people or things. The faithful also drink it at home, especially when unwell.

Horologion (Greek 'book of hours', Slavonic *chasoslov*)

The liturgical book containing the services and prayers for Compline, Mattins, Vespers and the different Hours of the day.

Hours

The short services of the day, kept especially in monasteries, whether in the church or in the monk's cell. They are First Hour (6.00 a.m.), Third Hour (9.00 a.m.), Sixth Hour (noon) and Ninth Hour (3.00 p.m.).

Idiorrhythmic

A form of monastic life in which monks follow an individual daily routine.

Kamilafki, *also* kalymauki (Slavonic *kamilavka*)

The black cylindrical hat worn by Orthodox clergy. *See also* **Epanokalymafkon.**

Kanon, see Canon

Kathisma

One of the twenty divisions of the Psalter.

Katholikon

The main church of a monastery.

Kliros

The section of the church dedicated to the choir. It was the practice of the Great Church, the Hagia Sophia in Constantinople, to have two choirs, one on each side of the church, and this practice became standard for all churches that followed the Byzantine typikon. The practice continues in larger churches, cathedrals, monasteries and seminaries, but more generally there is a single choir to one side of the solea or in a gallery.

Koinonikon

The hymn, varying with the day and the season, sung during communion.

Kolliva

A dish of boiled wheat kernels and other ingredients that is blessed at a memorial service and, following John 12.24, symbolizes resurrection.

Kolymbethra

A large circular basin on a stand, which is often moveable, containing the water for baptism by immersion.

Kontakion, *also* kondakion

A liturgical hymn that gives an abbreviated form of the meaning or history of the feast of a given day. The kontakion is sung after the sixth ode of the Canon in the Liturgy and the Service of the Hours.

Kulich

Easter bread, baked in tall, cylindrical tins and decorated with white icing. Traditionally blessed in decorated baskets with other Easter foods on Easter night, it is eaten before breakfast each day.

Kutya, see Kolliva

Lamb (Greek *amnos*)

The first square piece of bread taken from the prosphora which will be consecrated during the Eucharist and divided for communion.

Lance (Greek *lonche*, Slavonic *kopije*)

A triangular-ended double-edged knife used by the priest for cutting the altar bread during the service of Preparation of the Holy Gifts. A larger one is used to remove the Lamb, and a smaller one for the particles. It symbolizes the lance that pierced the side of Christ on the cross. *See also* **Proskomide**.

Litiya (Greek *artoklasia*)

The Slavonic term for the blessing of bread, wine, wheat and oil in the course of Vespers on special feasts. The bread soaked in wine is eaten later and the faithful are anointed on the forehead with the blessed oil.

Liturgy

In general, church services, including ceremonies, actions and gestures, accompanied by prayers and ritual objects. 'The Liturgy' usually refers to the celebration of the Eucharist.

Mandias

A long striped cloak, purple or blue in colour, worn by the bishop in various church ceremonies and services, such as Vespers, but not during the Liturgy.

Many Years, *see* Polychronion

Mattins, *also* Matins (Greek *orthros*, 'dawn')

The morning service which leads into the Liturgy. It begins with six psalms (*exapsalmos*), the reading of the Gospel, the chanting of the Canon and the Great Doxology.

Megalomartyr

A great or eminent martyr, given special veneration.

Megalynarion

The troparion sung at the commemoration of the Theotokos in the intercession following the consecration in the Liturgy. So called because of its connection to the Magnificat.

Memorial (Greek *mnymosyno*, Slavonic *panikhida*)

A service to pray for the repose of the souls of the dead, held on the third, ninth and fortieth day after death, after six months and after one or three years, or annually. Boiled wheat is used as a symbol of the general resurrection.

Menaion (from Greek 'month')

The name given to the twelve liturgical books containing the lives of the saints and the stichera for their commemorations.

Menologion

A collection of saints' lives arranged according to their commemoration in the church calendar.

Metania

Penitential prostrations made during private prayer or services. In the small metania the head and body are bowed; the great metania consists in kneeling and then, with both hands on the floor, bowing forward until the forehead touches the floor. Before kissing an icon it is usual to cross oneself and bow while touching the floor with one's right hand. This is done twice before kissing and once afterwards.

Metropolitan

The title of a bishop exercising provincial and not merely diocesan powers. Also conferred on senior bishops as an honorific title.

Mitre (Greek *mitra*)

The liturgical headdress or 'crown' of a bishop, the shape derived from Byzantine crowns. In Slavic churches archimandrites and archpriests are often allowed to wear a mitre. The mitre of a bishop has a cross on the top; the mitres of other clergy don't.

Moleben, *also* molieben

A Slavic service of supplication made in honour of Christ, the Theotokos or a particular saint or martyr. (The Greek equivalent is *Paraklesis*.)

Myrrh-bearing women

The women who brought spices to Christ's burial place on Easter morning and discovered the empty tomb.

Name-day (Greek *onomastiria*)

It is an Orthodox tradition to celebrate one's name-day instead of a birthday. The Orthodox are usually given the name of a saint at baptism; converts may have a 'church name' as well as a given name. Those with the same name celebrate together and greet one another, developing a special relationship with their patron saint.

Naos

The main worship space of a centrally planned Byzantine church.

Narthex

The vestibule area or porch of the church building, extending the width of the façade. Large buildings may have an outer narthex, known as the exonarthex.

Nave

Technically, the central aisle in a basilica, but often applied to the central area of a church building where the faithful stand or sit. *See* **Naos**.

Ode

Section of a canon, made up of a series of eight troparia, the first of which is called the hirmos. The number of troparia varies from canon to canon. The last ode of a canon is often addressed to the Theotokos. Each ode is devoted to an appropriate biblical text from the Old or New Testament.

Oktoechos (Greek 'eight modes')

Service book containing the canons and hymns in the eight tones or modes of Byzantine music, arranged on an eight-week cycle, one week for each tone.

Omophorion

A stole-like piece of embroidered white silk or velvet, about 25 centimetres (10 inches) wide, worn by bishops round the shoulder and falling loose towards the ground. There are two forms worn for the Liturgy: a larger one worn until the end of the Epistle, when it is laid aside prior to the reading of the Gospel, and a shorter one worn from the Cherubicon (the hymn sung during the Greater Entrance) until the end of the service.

Orarion

The deacon's stole. A silk band, worn over the left shoulder, and hanging straight down front and back; sometimes, before being left free to hang down in front, it is passed below the right arm, then attached once more to the left shoulder, and so hangs down in front. While reciting prayers, the deacon holds it in his hand. At the time of communion, it is crossed round the body.

Orthros (Greek 'dawn')

The name for the morning office which corresponds to Latin Mattins and Lauds. *See* **Mattins**.

Panagia (Greek 'All Holy')

1 One of the Orthodox titles of the Blessed Virgin Mary.
2 An icon depicting the Virgin Mary with the Christ-child.
3 A bishop's encolpion decorated with an icon of the Panagia.

Panikhida, see Memorial

Pantocrator

Greek term for the 'Lord who rules over all'. It is a title of the Son of God. In Orthodox art, 'Pantocrator' refers to the icon decorating the centre of the dome, depicting Christ as the almighty God and Lord of the Universe.

Pascha

Easter; the great feast of feasts, the Lord's Passover and Resurrection.

Paschal trikerion

A triple candlestick used at Easter. In the Slavic tradition, the three candleholders, with beeswax candles, are attached to a large blessing crucifix with a vertical handle. The trikerion is held by the priest and used for blessing. Fresh flowers are often attached to it.

Pashka

A festive Easter dish consisting primarily of foods prohibited during the Great Fast. The main ingredient is *tvorog* (curd cheese) with butter, eggs, sour cream and nuts, dried fruit and spices. Shaped as a truncated pyramid, it is decorated with symbols of Christ's Resurrection and served with *kulich*.

Pastophoria

The two chapels, the Prothesis and the Diakonikon, on the north and south sides of the sanctuary respectively.

Paten, see Diskos

Paterikon

A book detailing the lives of the saintly monks of a particular monastery.

Patriarch (Greek 'in charge of a family')

The highest prelate of an Orthodox church. Today they are eight in number. *See* **Patriarchate** and **Ecumenical Patriarch**.

Patriarchate

An ecclesiastical jurisdiction governed by a patriarch. There were five ancient patriarchates: Rome (acknowledged until the Great Schism of 1054), Constantinople, Antioch, Alexandria and Jerusalem. In addition, there are five Slavic patriarchates: Moscow, Bulgaria, Romania, Serbia and Georgia.

Pectoral cross

A cross of metal on a chain round the neck worn on the breast by archimandrites, archpriests and, in Russia, also by simple priests.

Pentecost (Greek 'fiftieth day')

The feast celebrated fifty days after Pascha, marking the descent of the Holy Spirit on the Apostles.

Pentecostarion

The liturgical book containing all the prayers, hymns and services for the period of fifty days between Pascha and Pentecost.

Phelonion (Greek *phelonion*, Slavonic *felon*)

The liturgical vestment proper to the priest. It is the Orthodox form of the Latin chasuble, a long, ample garment put on over the head, gathered in the front so that it looks more like a cope.

Pogrebeniye

Slavonic term for a funeral rite (Greek *taphe*).

Polychronion (Greek 'many years')

A prayer sung by the chanter or choir at the end of a service to honour a bishop or priest, asking for many years of life.

Polyeleos (Greek 'much mercy')

Psalms 134 and 135 (LXX) as the third reading of the Psalter at Mattins on Great Feasts, some Sundays and feasts of a certain rank. The name arises from the repetition of the phrase 'for His mercy endureth for ever'.

Polykandelon (Greek 'many lights')

A metal support, usually circular, cruciform or rectangular, for multiple glass oil lights, suspended in Byzantine churches.

Prayer rope (Greek *komboskini*, Slavonic *chotki*)

A loop of complex woven knots, usually made from wool or silk, used to count the recitations of the Jesus Prayer. It typically has thirty-three knots, representing the years of Christ's life, or a hundred.

Presanctified

A shorthand for the Liturgy of the Presanctified Gifts, being communion administered from the Gifts consecrated the previous Sunday. It is the only form allowed on weekdays in Lent and takes place on Wednesdays and Fridays. The rite is attributed to

Pope Gregory the Great, known in Orthodoxy as St Gregory the Dialogist, because he was the author of a book of dialogues.

Prokeimenon (Greek 'gradual introduction')

A liturgical verse or scriptural passage read or sung before the Apostle (Epistle) in the Liturgy.

Proskomide (Greek 'gathering of gifts', Slavonic *zhertvennik*)

The service of preparation of the bread and wine (the Holy Gifts) before the Liturgy which takes place at the Prothesis.

Prosphoro, prosphora (Greek 'offering gift')

The leavened altar bread made of pure wheat flour to be used for the Eucharist. The round loaves are stamped on the top with a special seal (*sphragis*) of a square divided by a cross into four smaller squares in which are severally inscribed IC, XC, NI, KA (meaning 'Jesus Christ conquers') or the corresponding letters in another liturgical language. That which is not used for the Eucharist is cut up for the antidoron.

Prostrations, *see* Metania

Prothesis

The Table of Preparation or Oblation, in a separate area north of the Holy Table or in the northeast corner of the sanctuary, is used for the preparation of the Holy Gifts of bread and wine for the Eucharist. It is similar to the Holy Table and covered in the same colour cloths. A single candle stands on the Table, together with the chalice, diskos, lance and spoon, the asterisk, the veils, and the sponge and cloths for drying the chalice after the Liturgy. Names for commemoration are also gathered here.

Reader (Greek *anagnostis*, Slavonic *chtets*)

The person assigned to read, chant and give responses in church services, who may be blessed by the bishop in a special ceremony.

Sakkos

A vestment similar in form to the Latin dalmatic, which originated in Byzantium and became part of the patriarch's vestments in the eleventh century. This garment had no sleeves and was donned over the head and buttoned on the sides. Originally limited to patriarchs, metropolitans and archbishops, it is now worn instead of the phelonion by all bishops. Small bells are attached to it.

Semantron

A bent iron bar which, when struck with a mallet, produces a high ringing sound. It is used to signal the beginning of services. Largely superseded by bells, their use persists in monastic communities. A wooden board used for this purpose is termed a talanton.

Skouphos

The soft black cap of a monk.

Solea

An elevated area in front of the iconostasis where various rites and ceremonies taken place.

Sponge, Holy

A small natural sponge used during the Liturgy to sweep together the particles on the paten, to sweep them off the paten into the chalice and to purify the sacred vessels after communion.

Staretz

The Russian word originally meant 'an old man'; it now refers to a spiritual guide distinguished by personal holiness, who is generally a monk but can be a lay man or woman.

Stavropegion

A monastery or community directly under the jurisdiction of the Ecumenical Patriarch.

Sticharion (Slavonic *stikhar*)

A liturgical tunic, usually of coloured stuff, comparable with the Western alb. It is worn as the undermost vestment by priests and deacons and is then usually white or gold, but can be the same colour as the phelonion. It is worn as an outer vestment by deacons, subdeacons and servers. It is open down the side and held by hook and eye, or equivalent. That of the deacon is long, ungirdled and wide-sleeved, resembling a Latin dalmatic.

Sticheron

A brief liturgical hymn attached to a verse (*stichos*) of a psalm or other passage of Scripture.

Subdeacon (Greek *hypodiakonos*)

A layman who has received a special blessing from the bishop to enable him to assist with services and ceremonies.

Synaxarion

A brief biography of a saint read on his or her feast day; also the book that contains brief lives of the saints for the entire year.

Synaxis (Greek 'assembly', Slavonic *sobor*)

1 A gathering of the faithful in honour of a saint, where the life is read from a synaxarion.
2 The liturgical office said by monks in common, usually on Saturday or Sunday.

Tabernacle (Greek *artophorion*, Slavonic *darochranitelnitsa*)

A receptacle on the Holy Table, often in the form of a church building, in which the consecrated Holy Gifts are preserved for the communion of the Sick or the Liturgy of the Presanctified Gifts during Lent.

Talanton

A board of hard cypress wood some six feet (nearly two metres) long, suspended from the middle by a cord, which gives a soft hammering sound when struck. It is used to call monastic communities to prayer. The metal equivalent is called a semantron.

Temple (Greek *naos*, Slavonic *khram*)

The usual word used among the Orthodox to refer to a church building.

Theotokion (Greek 'referring to the Theotokes', Slavonic *Bogorodichev*)

A hymn, troparion or sticheron, referring to the Theotokos.

Theotokos

The most frequently used title of the Blessed Virgin Mary; Greek for 'birth-giver/bearer of God'. The title was officially recognized at the Third Ecumenical Council at Ephesus, AD 431.

Throne, Holy

The Slavonic name for the Holy Table.

Trikerion, *see* Paschal trikerion

Triodion (Greek 'three odes')

The period of the church's year between the Sunday of the Publican and the Pharisee and Cheese-fare Sunday. Also, and more usually, the liturgical book containing hymns, prayers and services from the Sunday of the Publican and the Pharisee until Pascha.

Trisagion

One of the most ancient and most used hymns of the Orthodox Church: 'Holy God, Holy and Mighty, Holy and Immortal, have mercy upon us.' The term is also used to refer to a memorial service for the repose of a soul.

Troparion

The general name for the short hymns or verses in rhythmical prose of which the longer hymns are composed.

Typikon (Greek 'following the order', Slavonic *sluzhebnik*)

Rule of liturgical procedure or rule observed by a monastery. Also the liturgical book that contains instructions for ordering various church services and ceremonies in the form of a perpetual calendar.

Veils

Three veils are used to cover the sacred vessels during the Liturgy. The First Veil covers the paten and is supported, to keep it off the Lamb, by the asterisk. The Second Veil covers the chalice. The Third Veil is the aër, which covers both.

Vespers (Greek *hesperinos*, Slavonic *vechernia*)

The formal evening service of the Church.

Vestments (Greek *amphia*)

The distinctive garments worn by the clergy in the Liturgy and the other church services. Among them are cassock, epigonation, epitrachelion, omophorion, orarion, sakkos, sticharion and zone.

Vigil (Greek *olonychtia*)

Spiritual exercises during the night preceding the feast day of a saint or some other major feast, involving spiritual preparation, prayer and services.

Vladyka

Honorific title in Church Slavonic for a bishop. *Vladyka* is the nominative form used when referring to a bishop in the third person; *Vladyko* is vocative, used when addressing the bishop directly, such as in the Liturgy.

Xerophagy

Literally 'dry eating' during a fast – that is, vegetables cooked with water and salt, together with fruit, nuts, bread and honey.

Zapivka (Slavonic 'washing down')

Wine diluted with warm water that is drunk after receiving communion (in the Russian Orthodox Church), followed by eating the antidoron. Its purpose is that of washing any remnants of communion from the mouth.

Zeon (Greek 'boiling')

Hot water that is blessed and added to the chalice by the priest before the communion of the people. It signifies the 'living warmth' of the Holy Spirit. Some Byzantine commentators say that it represents the water that flowed from the side of Christ on the cross when He was pierced by a spear.

Zone, see Girdle

Text sources

Throughout the book

Liturgical and prayer books (as listed in the select bibliography); *The Philokalia*; McGuckin, *The Orthodox Church* (cited as McGuckin); Ware, *The Orthodox Church* (cited as Ware); Cunningham and Theokritoff, *The Cambridge Companion to Orthodox Christian Theology* (cited as CCOCT).

1 Blessed is our God

<http://journeytoorthodoxy.com/2013/01/mother-theklas-letter-to-a-new-convert>; John of Damascus, *Writings*; Bettenson, *Later Christian Fathers*; Cyril of Jerusalem, *Catechetical Lectures*; Athanasius, *On the Incarnation*; Cabasilas, *Commentary*; Postnikov, *How to Live a Holy Life*; Schmemann, *For the Life of the World*; Louth, *Modern Orthodox Thinkers*; Lash in CCOTC; Bulgakov, 'Dogma and dogmatic theology'; Fedotov, *Treasury of Russian Spirituality*; Lossky, *The Mystical Theology of the Eastern Church*; Ward, *The Sayings of the Desert Fathers*; McGuckin.

2 The Orthodox ethos

John of Damascus, *Writings*; Ousterhout, 'The Holy Space'; Likhachev, 'Russian Orthodoxy'; Smith, *The Volokolamsk Paterikon*; Ward, *The Sayings of the Desert Fathers;* Porphyrios, *Wounded by Love*; Boersma, *Embodiment and Virtue in Gregory of Nyssa*; Rounding, *Alix and Nicky*.

3 The wedding garment

Athanasius, *Letter to Marcellinus*; Chrysostom, *On Repentance and Almsgiving*; Cyril of Jerusalem, *Catechetical Lectures*; Gregory the Great, *Forty Gospel Homilies*; Augustine, *Homilies on the Gospels*;

Leo the Great, *Epistles*; *The Philokalia*; Photius, *Homilies*; Ward, *The Sayings of the Desert Fathers*; Fedotov, *The Russian Religious Mind*; Lossky, *Dogmatic Theology*; Nellas, *Deification in Christ*; Mother Marina, *To the Glory of the Holy Trinity*.

4 Heaven on earth

Ousterhout, 'The Holy Space'; Mathewes-Green, *Welcome to the Orthodox Church*; Kuvochinsky (trans.), *Divine Liturgy*; Leskov, *The Cathedral Clergy*; Hammond, *The Waters of Marah*; St Tikhon's, *These Truths We Hold*.

5 The holy icons

Kartsonis, 'The responding icon'; Bulgakov, *Icons and the Name of God*; Runciman, *The Fall of Constantinople*; Greenfield and Talbot, *Holy Men of Mount Athos*; Heppell, *Paterik*; Smith, *The Volokolamsk Paterikon*; Ouspensky, *Theology of the Icon*; Archimandrite Sergei, *Treasures of Valamo Monastery*; CCOTC, 'Theology of the icon'; Woolf, 'Footnote to an incident . . .'

6 The Holy Liturgy

The Divine Liturgy (various editions including Thyateira, Jordanville and Brightman); Woolfenden, *A Practical Handbook*; Nicholas Cabasilas, *Commentary*; Riley, *Guide to the Divine Liturgy in the East*.

7 Music and musicians

Boersma, *Embodiment and Virtue in Gregory of Nyssa*; Maes, *History of Russian Sacred Music*; von Gardner, *Russian Church Singing*; Mann, *Russian Sacred Music for Choirs*; von Meck, 'To My Best Friend'; Tavener, *The Music of Silence*; Bouteneff, *Arvo Pärt*.

8 Orthodoxy and literature

Bulgakov, *Churchly Joy*; Obolensky, *The Penguin Book of Russian Verse*; Mirsky, *History of Russian Literature*; Blanch, *Journey into the Mind's Eye*; Bely, *Petersburg*; Chekhov, *Stories*; Lermontov,

A Hero of Our Time; Leskov, *The Cathedral Clergy*; Pushkin, *Love Poems*; Teffi, *Rasputin and Other Ironies*; Pasternak, *Dr Zhivago*.

9 Fasting, confession and prayer

Evagrius Ponticus, *The Praktikos*; *The Philokalia*; Fedotov, *The Russian Religious Mind*; Chariton, *The Art of Prayer*; John of Valamo, *God is in Our Midst*; Men, *An Inner Step*; Deseille, *La Spiritualité Orthodoxe*; Panteleimon, *A Star in the Heavens*; Paul of Finland, *The Faith We Hold*; Rounding, *Catherine the Great*; Schmemann, *For the Life of the World*; Ware, in *Lenten Triodion*; Ware, *The Power of the Name*.

10 The resurrection life

McGuckin; John Climacus; John of Valamo; *The Pentecostarion*.

Appendix 1 The Orthodox church year

Woolfenden, *A Practical Handbook*; Bobrinskoy, *La Vie Liturgique*.

Appendix 2 An Orthodox glossary

Arseni, *Ortodoksinen sanasto*; Brightman, *The Divine Liturgy*; McGuckin; Ware; Safran (ed.), *Heaven on Earth*; Bulgaris, *The Holy Catechism*; Larchet, *Theology of the Body*; André Lossky, sleeve notes to *Russian Easter Liturgy*; Hapgood (trans.), *Service Book of the Holy Orthodox–Catholic Apostolic (Greco-Russian) Church*; *The Pentecostarion*.

Select bibliography

Liturgical and prayer books

Prayer Book, Jordanville, New York: Holy Trinity Monastery, 4th edn, 2011

Orthodox Daily Prayers (edited by Sergei D. Arhipov), South Canaan, Pennsylvania: St Tikhon's Seminary Press, e-book edition, 2014

Vsenoshchnoe bdenie, Chasy, Bozhestvennaya Liturgiya, Moscow: Sibirskaya Blagozvonnitsa Artos-Media, 2009

Service Book of the Holy Orthodox–Catholic Apostolic (Greco-Russian) Church (translated by Isabel Florence Hapgood), Boston, Massachusetts: Houghton, Mifflin & Co., 1906

Service Books of the Orthodox Church (The Divine Liturgies of St John Chrysostom and St Basil the Great and the Liturgy of the Presanctified Gifts), South Canaan, Pennsylvania: St Tikhon's Monastery Press, e-book edition, 2014

The Divine Liturgy of Saint John Chrysostom (translated by F. E. Brightman), London: The Faith Press, 1922

The Divine Liturgy of Our Father among the Saints John Chrysostom (Greek–English; translated by Archimandrite Ephrem Lash), London: The Greek Orthodox Archdiocese of Thyateira and Great Britain, 2011

The Divine Liturgy of Our Father among the Saints John Chrysostom (Slavonic–English), Jordanville, New York: Holy Trinity Monastery, 4th edn, 2015

The Divine Liturgy of the Holy Orthodox Catholic Apostolic Græco-Russian Church (translated from Slavonic by P. Kuvochinsky), London: Cope and Fenwick, 1909

The Festal Menaion (translated by Mother Mary and Kallistos Ware), South Canaan, Pennsylvania: St Tikhon's Seminary Press, 1998

The Lenten Triodion (translated by Mother Mary and Kallistos Ware), South Canaan, Pennsylvania: St Tikhon's Seminary Press, 2002

The Lenten Triodion Supplementary Texts (translated by Mother Mary and Kallistos Ware), South Canaan, Pennsylvania: St Tikhon's Seminary Press, 2007

The Great Horologion or Book of Hours, Boston, Massachusetts: Holy Transfiguration Monastery, 1997

The Pentecostarion, Boston, Massachusetts: Holy Transfiguration Monastery, 2014

The Philokalia: The complete text compiled by St Nikodimos of the Holy Mountain and St Makarios of Corinth (translated by G. E. H. Palmer, Philip Sherrard and Kallistos Ware), London: Faber, 1979 (vol. 1), 1981 (vol. 2), 1984 (vol. 3), 1995 (vol. 4)

Fathers, spiritual writers, paterika

Athanasius	*The Incarnation of the Word of God* (translated by a religious of CSMV), London: G. Bles, The Centenary Press, 1944
Athanasius	*The Life of Anthony and The Letter to Marcellinus*, Mahwah, New Jersey: Paulist Press, 1980 (The Classics of Western Spirituality)
Athos, Holy Men of	*Holy Men of Mount Athos* (edited and translated by Richard P. H. Greenfield and Alice-Mary Talbot), Cambridge, Massachusetts: Harvard University Press, 2016
Augustine	*Homilies on the Gospels*, Volume 6, in *A Select Library of the Nicene and Post-Nicene Fathers of the Christian Church*, first series (edited by Philip Schaff), Grand Rapids, Michigan: Eerdmanns, 1956

Augustine   *Confessions* (translated by R. S. Pine-Coffin), Harmondsworth: Penguin, 1961

Cyril of Jerusalem   *Catechetical Lectures*, in *The Library of Christian Classics, Volume IV, Cyril of Jerusalem and Nemesius of Edessa*, London: SCM Press, 1955

Evagrius Ponticus   *The Praktikos and Chapters on Prayer* (translation, introduction and notes by John Eudes Bamberger OCSO), Trappist, Kentucky: Cistercian Publications, 1972

Gregory the Great   *Forty Gospel Homilies* (translated by David Hurst OSB), Kalamazoo, Michigan: Cistercian Publications, 1990

Leo the Great   *Epistles*, Volume XII, in *A Select Library of the Nicene and Post-Nicene Fathers of the Christian Church*, second series, Grand Rapids, Michigan: Eerdmans 1976

John Chrysostom   *Commentary on the Psalms* (translated by R. C. Hill), two volumes, Brookline, Massachusetts: Holy Cross Orthodox Press, 1998

John Chrysostom   *On Repentance and Almsgiving* (translated by G. G. Christo), Washington, DC: Catholic University of America Press, 1998

John Climacus   *The Ladder of Divine Ascent*, Toronto: Patristic Publishing, 2017

John of Damascus   *Writings* (translated by F. H. Chase), Washington, DC: Catholic University of America Press, 1958

Nicholas Cabasilas   *A Commentary on the Divine Liturgy*, London: SPCK, 1960

Niketas Stethatos   *The Life of Saint Symeon the New Theologian* (translated by R. P. H.

	Greenfield), Cambridge, Massachusetts: Harvard University Press, 2013
Photius	*The Homilies of Photius Patriarch of Constantinople* (English translation, introduction and commentary by Cyril Mango), Cambridge, Massachusetts: Harvard University Press, 1958
Symeon of Thessalonika	*The Liturgical Commentaries* (edited and translated by S. Hawkes-Teeples), Toronto: Pontifical Institute of Medieval Studies, 2011

Other books

Anonymous	*Hungry Orthodox Christian Reader: The hidden writings of Orthodox Christianity*, Chicago, Illinois: OLGA Press, 2015
Anonymous	*The Way of a Pilgrim* (translated by Anna Zaranko, edited by Andrew Louth), Harmondsworth: Penguin, 2017
Arseni, Arkkimandritta	*Ortodoksinen sanasto*, Helsinki: Otava, 1999
Bely, Andrei	*Petersburg* (translated by John Elsworth), London: Pushkin Press, 2009
Bettenson, Henry S.	*Later Christian Fathers*, Oxford: Oxford University Press, 1970
Blanch, Lesley	*Journey into the Mind's Eye*, London: Collins, 1968
Bobrinskoy, Boris	*La Vie Liturgique*, Paris: Cerf, 2000
Boersma, Hans	*Embodiment and Virtue in Gregory of Nyssa: An anagogical approach*, Oxford: Oxford University Press, 2013
Bolshakoff, Sergius	*Russian Mystics*, Kalamazoo, Michigan: Cistercian Publications, 1980
Bouteneff, Peter C.	*Arvo Pärt: Out of silence*, Yonkers, New

	York: St Vladimir's Seminary Press, 2015
Bulgakov, Sergei	'Dogma and dogmatic theology', in Michael Plekon (editor), *Tradition Alive: On the Church and the Christian life in our time*, Lanham, Maryland: Sheed & Ward, 2003
Bulgakov, Sergei	*Churchly Joy: Orthodox devotions for the church year* (translated by Boris Jakim), Grand Rapids, Michigan: Eerdmans, 2008
Bulgakov, Sergius	*Icons and the Name of God*, Grand Rapids, Michigan: Eerdmans, 2012
Bulgaris, Nicolas	*The Holy Catechism* (translated by W. E. Daniel, edited by R. R. Bromage), London: Masters, 1893
Chariton, Igumen	*The Art of Prayer: An Orthodox anthology*, London: Faber and Faber, 1966
Chekhov, Anton	*Stories* (translated by Richard Pevear and Larissa Volokhonsky), New York: Bantam, 2000
Clendenin, Daniel B.	*Eastern Orthodox Theology: A contemporary reader*, 2nd edn, Grand Rapids, Michigan: Baker Academic, 2003
Cunningham, Elizabeth, and Theokritoff, Mary B.	*The Cambridge Companion to Orthodox Christian Theology*, Cambridge: Cambridge University Press, 2008
Deseille, Placide	*La Spiritualité Orthodoxe et la Philocalie*, Paris: Bayard Éditions, 1997
Fedotov, George P.	*The Russian Religious Mind: Kievan Christianity*, Cambridge, Massachusetts: Harvard University Press, 1946
Fedotov, George P.	*A Treasury of Russian Spirituality*, London: Sheed & Ward, 1950

Gardner, Johann von — *Russian Church Singing, Volume 1: Orthodox Worship and Hymnography*, Crestwood, New York: St Vladimir's Seminary Press, 1980

Gogol, Nikolai — *Meditations on the Divine Liturgy*, Jordanville: Holy Trinity Publications, 3rd edn, 2014

Greenfield, Richard P. H. and Talbot, Alice-Mary (translators) — *Holy Men of Mount Athos*, Cambridge, Massachusetts: Harvard University Press, 2016

Hammond, Peter — *The Waters of Marah: The present state of the Greek church*, London: Rockliff, 1956

Heppell, Muriel (translator) — *The Paterik of the Kievan Caves Monastery*, Cambridge, Massachusetts: Ukrainian Research Institute of Harvard University, 1989

John of Valamo, Father — *Christ is in Our Midst*, London: Darton, Longman & Todd, 1980

Kartsonis, Anna — 'The responding icon', in Linda Safran (editor), *Heaven on Earth: Art and the Church in Byzantium*, University Park, Pennsylvania: Pennsylvania State University Press, 1998

Kohonen, Niilo (editor) — *Valamo and its Message*, Helsinki: Valamo-Seura, 1983

Larchet, Jean-Claude — *Theology of the Body*, Yonkers, New York: St Vladimir's Seminary Press, 2016

Lermontov, Mikhail — *A Hero of Our Time* (translated by Paul Foote), Harmondsworth: Penguin, 1966

Leskov, Nikolay — *The Cathedral Clergy* (translation and introduction by Margaret Winchell), Bloomington, Indiana: Slavica, 2010

Likhachev, Dmitry, and Rzhevsky, Nicholas
'Religion: Russian Orthodoxy' in N. Rzhevsky (ed.), *The Cambridge Companion to Modern Russian Culture*, Cambridge: Cambridge University Press, 2001

Lossky, André
'Short glossary of liturgical terms', in notes to the Opus 111 recording *Russian Easter Liturgy: The Easter Canon of St John Damascene*, Paris, 1995

Lossky, Vladimir
The Mystical Theology of the Eastern Church (translated by members of the Fellowship of St Alban and St Sergius), London: J. Clarke, 1957

Lossky, Vladimir
Dogmatic Theology: Creation, God's image in man, and the redeeming work of the Trinity, Yonkers, New York: St Vladimir's Seminary Press, 2017

Louth, Andrew
Modern Orthodox Thinkers: From the Philokalia to the present, London: SPCK, 2015

Luehrmann, Sonja (editor)
Praying with the Senses: Contemporary Orthodox Christian spirituality in practice, Bloomington, Indiana: Indiana University Press, 2018

McGuckin, John Anthony
The Orthodox Church: An introduction to its history, doctrine, and spiritual culture. Chichester: Wiley-Blackwell, 2011

Maes, Francis
A History of Russian Sacred Music, Berkeley, California: University of California Press, 1996

Mann, Noëlle
Russian Sacred Music for Choirs, Oxford: Oxford University Press, 2013

Marina, Mother
To the Glory of the Holy Trinity: A year in the life of the convent of Lintula, Helsinki: Valamo Monastery, 1995

Mathewes-Green, Frederica	*Welcome to the Orthodox Church: An introduction to Eastern Christianity*, Brewster, Massachusetts: Paraclete Press, 2015
Meck, Galina von (translator)	*'To My Best Friend': Correspondence between Tchaikovsky and Nadezhda von Meck 1876–1878*, Oxford: Oxford University Press, 1993
Men, Alexander	*An Inner Step Toward God: Father Alexander Men's writings and teachings on prayer*, Brewster, Massachusetts: Paraclete Press, 2014
Mirsky, D. S.	*A History of Russian Literature*, London: Routledge & Kegan Paul, 1968
Nellas, Panayiotis	*Deification in Christ: Orthodox perspectives on the nature of the human person* (translated by Norman Russell), Crestwood, New York: St Vladimir's Seminary Press, 1987
Obolensky, Dimitri	*The Penguin Book of Russian Verse*, Harmondsworth: Penguin, 1965
Ouspensky, Leonid	*Theology of the Icon* (two volumes, translated by Anthony Gythiel), Crestwood, New York: St Vladimir's Seminary Press, 1992
Ousterhout, Robert	'The Holy Space', in Linda Safran (editor), *Heaven on Earth: Art and the Church in Byzantium*, University Park, Pennsylvania: Pennsylvania State University Press, 1998
Panteleimon, Archimandrite	*A Star in the Heavens: The life of Father John of Valamo*, Valamo: Valamo Monastery, 1991
Pasternak, Boris	*Dr Zhivago* (translated by Max Hayward and Manya Harari), London: Collins, 1958

Paul of Finland, Archbishop	*The Faith We Hold*, Crestwood, New York: St Vladimir's Seminary Press, 1999
Porphyrios, St	*Wounded by Love: The life and wisdom of Saint Porphyrios*, Limni, Evia, Greece: Denise Harvey, 2005
Postnikov, Gregory	*How to Live a Holy Life* (translated from the Russian by Seraphim F. Englehardt), Jordanville, New York: Holy Trinity Publications, 2012
Pushkin, Alexander	*Love Poems* (edited by Roger Clarke), Richmond: Alma Classics, 2016
Riley, Athelstan	*A Guide to the Divine Liturgy in the East*, London: Mowbray, 1922
Rounding, Virginia	*Catherine the Great*, London: Hutchinson, 2006
Rounding, Virginia	*Alix and Nicky*, New York: St Martin's Press, 2011
Runciman, Steven	*The Fall of Constantinople, 1453*, Cambridge: Cambridge University Press, 1969
Safran, Linda (editor)	*Heaven on Earth: Art and the Church in Byzantium*, University Park, Pennsylvania: Pennsylvania State University Press, 1998
St Tikhon's, a monk of	*These Truths We Hold: The Holy Orthodox Church: Her life and teachings*, South Canaan, Pennsylvania: St Tikhon's Monastery Press, 1986
Schmemann, Alexander	*For the Life of the World: Sacraments and Orthodoxy*, Crestwood, New York: St Vladimir's Seminary Press, 1973
Sergei, Archimandrite	*Treasures of Valamo Monastery*, Valamo: Valamo Monastery, 2012
Smith, T. Allan	*The Volokolamsk Paterikon: A window on a Muscovite monastery*, Toronto:

	Pontifical Institute of Medieval Studies, 2008
Tavener, John	*The Music of Silence: A composer's testament*, London: Faber and Faber, 1999
Teffi	*Rasputin and Other Ironies* (translated from the Russian by Robert Chandler, Elizabeth Chandler, Rose France and Anne Marie Jackson), London: Pushkin Press, 2016
Tolstoy, Leo	*The Death of Ivan Illich and Other Stories* (translated by Richard Pevear and Larissa Volokhonsky), London: Vintage, 2010
Vasileos, Archimandrite	*Hymn of Entry*, Crestwood, New York: St Vladimir's Seminary Press, 1984
Ward, Benedicta	*The Sayings of the Desert Fathers: The alphabetical collection* (translated by Benedicta Ward), London: Mowbrays, 1975
Ware, Kallistos (Timothy)	*The Orthodox Church*, Harmondsworth: Penguin, 1963
Ware, Kallistos	*The Power of the Name: The Jesus Prayer in Orthodox spirituality*, Oxford: SLG Press, 1977
Wolff, Robert Lee	'Footnote to an incident of the Latin occupation of Constantinople: the Church and Icon of the Hodegetria', *Traditio* 6 (1948): 319–28.
Woolfenden, Gregory	*A Practical Handbook for Divine Services*, Jordanville, New York: Holy Trinity Publications, 2011

Further reading

John Anthony McGuckin, *The Orthodox Church: An introduction to its history, doctrine, and spiritual culture* (Chichester: Wiley-Blackwell, 2011) is a more comprehensive book than its title suggests. Though its 450 pages would have been much improved by page subheadings to guide the reader and a decent index for reference, it is the best single-volume work available.

There are many differences between European and American versions of Orthodoxy, but there is much to be gained from Frederica Mathewes-Green's excellent and accessible book *Welcome to the Orthodox Church: An introduction to Eastern Christianity* (Brewster, Massachusetts: Paraclete Press, 2015), especially if one is seriously considering becoming Orthodox. She does a brilliant job in explaining what it is like to belong to an Orthodox community, albeit one that worships in English in America.

An extraordinarily mind-stretching guide to the possibilities of Orthodox reading is provided by Orthodox Literary Growth Advocates' *Hungry Orthodox Christian Reader: The hidden writings of Orthodox Christianity* (Chicago, Illinois: OLGA Press, 2015), which is a sampler of all sorts of writings – Fathers, mystics, lives of saints, liturgical texts and sermons, with a helpful chapter listing all the writings published in various series (Ancient Christian Writers, Cistercian Publications, Classics of Western Spirituality, Fathers of the Church, Ante-Nicene Fathers, Nicene and Post-Nicene Fathers). The latter two series are freely available on the web and for a modest cost available as e-books. An extraordinary number of modern translations of the Fathers are available. John Chrysostom's homilies remain very fresh thanks to Gus George Christo's lively translation of *St John Chrysostom on Repentance and Almsgiving* (Washington, DC: Catholic University of America Press, 1998) and to Robert Charles Hill's two volumes of Chrysostom's *Commentary on the Psalms* (Brookline, Massachusetts: Holy Cross Orthodox Press, 1998)

The history of the Orthodox Church in the twentieth century and the problems that have continued into the current century are much illuminated by a great work of archival scholarship by a Bulgarian scholar, Daniela Kalkandjieva, *The Russian Orthodox Church, 1917–1948* (Abingdon: Routledge, 2015).

It is the subtitle that reveals the true value of *Praying with the Senses: Contemporary Orthodox Christian spirituality in practice* (Bloomington, Indiana: Indiana University Press, 2018), edited by anthropologist Sonja Luehrmann. This book brings together a series of fascinating studies of Orthodoxy as it is lived today.

There are a number of learned commentaries on the Divine Liturgy that will attract scholars. The edition of St Symeon of Thessalonika's *The Liturgical Commentaries*, edited and translated by Steven Hawkes-Teeples (Toronto: Pontifical Institute of Medieval Studies, 2011), with Greek and English in parallel, is readable and enjoyable for specialist and non-specialist alike. Nikolai Gogol's delightful and informative *Meditations on the Divine Liturgy* (Jordanville, New York: Holy Trinity Publications, 2014), completed in 1851, have been helpfully updated by use of the 2013 edition of the Jordanville version of the Divine Liturgy of St John Chrysostom.

I continue to value the writings of George P. Fedotov and I would recommend *The Russian Religious Mind: Kievan Christianity*, which, though published in 1946, is still available. (This is Volume 1; I would not recommend Volume 2, which Fedotov left unfinished on his death.) He also produced a useful anthology, previously entitled *A Treasury of Russian Spirituality* and reissued as *The Way of a Pilgrim and Other Classics of Russian Spirituality*. The best little book on the Jesus Prayer is still that by Metropolitan Kallistos of Diokleia, *The Power of the Name: The Jesus Prayer in Orthodox spirituality*, which is available as an e-book.

A number of more recent spiritual leaders deserve attention. Archimandrite Vasileos's book *Hymn of Entry* (Crestwood, New York: St Vladimir's Seminary Press, 1984) requires slow and attentive reading. There is much to be gained, in knowledge and enjoyment, from reading the readily available *Wounded by Love: The life and wisdom of Saint Porphyrios* (Limni, Evia, Greece: Denise Harvey, 2005), to which I have already referred, and *Monastic Wisdom: The letters of Elder Joseph the Hesychast* (Florence, Arizona: St Anthony's Greek Orthodox Monastery, 1998).

It has not been possible to discuss modern Orthodox theology in this book, though it has been informed by it. Andrew Louth's *Modern Orthodox Thinkers: From the Philokalia to the present* (London: SPCK, 2015) is an engaging lecture course packaged in a book leading the reader to an understanding of the development of Orthodox theology through the last century and an engagement with the writings of many Orthodox thinkers. It repays frequent rereading.

Index

Index

Index